PENGUIN BOOKS

POLITICS IS FOR PEOPLE

Shirley Williams was born in 1930, daughter of George Catlin, the political scientist, and Vera Brittain, the author. She read philosophy, politics and economics at the University of Oxford, and was a Smith-Mundt Scholar at Columbia University, New York. She was married to Bernard Williams from 1955 until 1974 and she has a daughter, Rebecca Clare.

In 1964 she was elected to the House of Commons as the Labour Member for Hitchin, was immediately appointed Parliamentary Private Secretary to the Minister of Health and then Parliamentary Secretary to the Ministry of Labour. In 1967 she became Minister of State at the Department of Education and Science, and from 1969 to 1970 she was Minister of State at the Home Office. Between 1970 and 1974 she was opposition spokesman for social services, home affairs and prices, from 1974 to 1976 Secretary of State for Prices and Consumer Protection, and from 1976 to 1979, Secretary of State for Education and Science and Paymaster-General. She was a member of the National Executive of the Labour Party from 1970 to 1981 and has been since 1979 a research fellow at the Policy Studies Institute. She was a Visiting Fellow at Nuffield College, Oxford, from 1968 to 1975, Fellow of the Institute of Politics at the Kennedy School of Government during 1979–80, and Godkin Lecturer at Harvard University and Rede Lecturer at the University of Cambridge in 1980. She has received many academic honours, including doctorates from the universities of Leeds, Radcliffe (USA) and Leuven. She had her own discussion programme on BBC television, *Shirley Williams in Conversation*, during 1979.

Shirley Williams

Politics is for People

Penguin Books

Penguin Books Ltd, Harmondsworth, Middlesex, England
Penguin Books, 625 Madison Avenue, New York, New York 10022, U.S.A.
Penguin Books Australia Ltd, Ringwood, Victoria, Australia
Penguin Books Canada Ltd, 2801 John Street, Markham, Ontario, Canada L3R 1B4
Penguin Books N.Z.) Ltd, 182-190 Wairau Road, Auckland 10, New Zealand

First published 1981
Published simultaneously by Allen Lane

Made and printed in Great Britain by
Richard Clay (The Chaucer Press) Ltd, Bungay, Suffolk
Set in Monophoto Baskerville by
Northumberland Press Ltd, Gateshead, Tyne and Wear

FOR BECKY AND TIM

MY HOPES FOR THE FUTURE

Contents

List of Tables

Acknowledgements

My first debt is to Harvard University, under whose aegis the first part of this book was written. I worked in the autumn of 1979 at the Institute of Politics which is part of the Kennedy School of Government. The first two chapters emerged in lecture form as the 1980 Godkin Lectures, which I delivered at Harvard in April of that year. I am grateful for the ideas, thoughts and challenges of many friends at Harvard, who will permit me to single out in particular Dick and Bert Neustadt, Don Price, Graham Allison, Jonathan Moore, Carol Cerf and Bob Choate.

My second debt is to the Policy Studies Institute of London, which provided me with a warm welcome and a friendly atmosphere in which to work when I was defeated in the constituency of Hertford and Stevenage in May 1979. I have learned a lot from my fellow researchers and from the excellent lunchtime seminars, but again my PSI colleagues will not mind if I record particular thanks for their help and advice on this book to John Pinder, the Director, and Dick Davies, the Administrative Director. Some of the material in Chapters 6 and 7 first appeared in a PSI pamphlet, *Jobs for the Eighties*; part of Chapter 11, on education, was originally published in the National Union of Teachers' journal, *Secondary Education*, in the twenty-fifth anniversary issue, and part of Chapter 3 appeared in the Rede Lecture on 'Employment, Technology and Change', given at the University of Cambridge in November 1980.

I am deeply grateful to my friends, Stella Greenall, John Spencer and Anthony King, for their detailed criticism and comments on the book and I am also much indebted to Bill Daniel, Rudolf Klein,

Jim Northcott, Eileen Reid and Fritz Scharpf for help and comment on individual chapters. I owe Chris Brooks a great deal both for his ideas and for help with research material. I have tried to take almost everything they have said into account but I recognize that the attempt has not succeeded in correcting the book's shortcomings, for which I am alone responsible. I am grateful to my nephew Timothy Brittain-Catlin for his extraordinary persistence in digging out references and sources of quotations and to Michael Dixon for patient help with the proofs. Michele Bailleux, my secretary, has shown unremitting patience and understanding in turning scrawled and misshapen manuscripts into the semblance of order. Many other people have contributed ideas, criticisms or comments, and to them also I express my thanks.

For permission to quote from *High Windows* (1974) by Philip Larkin, I am grateful to Faber and Faber Ltd.

Introduction

For four of the last six years I have been engulfed in the work of government. Anyone who has ever been a minister or the leader of a large local authority knows that the job leaves little time for thought. One lives on the dwindling resources of past reading and past thinking. But if one doesn't think much, one does learn a good deal about the difficulties of governing, especially in a country like Britain, which is pluralistic and has tough-rooted institutions with a strong resistance to change. I began to feel that Britain's problems were largely institutional, and that her institutions have bred attitudes, especially class attitudes, that militate against a common effort to resolve her problems. The institutions, most of them intended to improve the quality of human life, have become bastions for particular interests against those of society as a whole. Political parties have been used as the instruments of one group of institutions or another, for example business or trades unions or professional groups.

Britain's problems seem especially serious because Britain has been less successful in coping with them than most other Western nations, perhaps because she has been protected for centuries from the horrors of invasion, occupation and destruction experienced by most continental European countries, which instilled in them the momentum for radical change. But Britain's problems are insignificant compared to those of the Third World, or even those of the Soviet bloc. The title of this book, *Politics is for People*, is not intended to refer only to the British people, but to the thousands of millions of people in our troubled and interdependent world.

I do not know whether the democratic political parties of the West can leap across the gulf between their current preoccupations and the world's circumstances. If they fail to do so, more and more people will become apathetic or else pursue the instant solutions offered by the fanatics of religion or politics. If they succeed, the exciting job could begin of creating a society for the individuals who live in it, rather than for the state, or capital, or technological progress. Either way, we are in for a turbulent decade.

I

The Achievement

In the thirty years after the end of the Second World War the politics of Western Europe were the politics of welfare democracy. A broad spectrum ranging from social democrats to Christian democrats and even to the progressive wing of the British Conservatives supported the welfare state, relatively high taxation together with some redistribution of income, and a mixed economy, though the proportion of publicly and privately owned industry within that mixed economy was a matter for fierce debate. Liberal democrats in the United States held similar views and pursued similar aims. Indeed welfare democracy and the Keynesian economics associated with it reigned almost unchallenged. In the harsher and more extreme climate of the 1980s, it has become fashionable to scorn that consensus. But it brought about – or at the very least coincided with – the highest standard of life ever experienced by ordinary men and women anywhere in the world.

Welfare democracy was based upon, indeed assumed, steady economic growth. Economic growth in turn depended upon abundant and cheap resources of energy, raw materials and land. Now these resources are becoming scarce and expensive. The prerequisites for rapid economic growth no longer exist. But without economic growth, what happens to a politics based on the promise of higher material standards for the people? Election after election, post-war politics has been about which party could promise and deliver higher material standards. Left-wing parties usually argued that public services should grow faster than private consumption;

right-wing parties argued to the contrary. Now, however, the very foundation of the debate is shattered.

So politics is in disarray. Some insist on regarding what is happening as a temporary dislocation which will be corrected before long, as if the world economy had pulled a muscle. This is the position of many middle-of-the-road moderate politicians, social democrat and progressive conservative alike. A second group argue that our current discontents stem from mistaken policies in the past, in particular too high a level of public spending and too large a role for the state: these are the monetarists and the conservatives. A third group, mainly on the left, hold the capitalist system responsible. It has broken down, and must now be replaced by some form of revolutionary socialism; these are Trotskyites, Marxist revolutionaries, far left socialists and the Western Communist parties, though with varying degrees of enthusiasm in this latter case.

Yet none of these analyses goes deep enough. For the changes we are seeing, in a time of such turbulence that our traditional institutions are being shaken to their roots, are not temporary. Nor are they simply the product of past policy mistakes, though these have made their contribution. They cannot even be attributed to one system, capitalist or communist, for both systems are visibly cracking under the stress. The crisis is a crisis of industrialism itself.

It is the thesis of this book that politicians, and in particular those like me who believe in social democracy, will have to make a quantum jump in their thinking, a leap to a new approach, if the West is to move forward from the achievements of the post-war years.

Socialism was a response to the particular kind of class structure created by the Industrial Revolution. It was primarily a European philosophy, only later picked up on other continents. But the modern post-industrial economy is very different from nineteenth-century industrialism. A declining minority of the population is employed in factories, the birthplace of the industrial proletariat. More and more people are in white-collar and professional jobs. A traditional socialism steeped in old industrial attitudes and based on the class war has become obsolete – a once useful but now unadaptable species in the evolution of politics. Before, however, I contemplate the leap in radical thinking that is required, let me say something about the starting point, the nature and achievement of welfare democracy.

THE ECONOMIC ACHIEVEMENT

The post-war goals of social democracy and, in the United States and Canada, of progressive liberalism, were the goals of economic growth, full employment, the abolition of poverty and equality of opportunity. They were perhaps best described by William Beveridge in 1942 when he said, 'The object of government in peace and in war is not the glory of rulers or of races, but the happiness of the common man.'[1] The methods that were adopted to achieve those goals constituted a substantial armoury. Government planning, public finance and government intervention were used to bring about and sustain full employment and economic growth; deficit financing maintained demand during periods of recession, themselves mild enough. The lessons of Maynard Keynes, set out in *The General Theory of Employment, Interest and Money*,[2] had been devotedly learned. The economy was largely controlled through these means, though in several Western European countries, especially Britain, France and Italy, public ownership of key industries or sectors of key industries was a major instrument too. Most Western European industrialized countries had ceased to be purely capitalist economies early in the twentieth century, but the size of the public sector had been small and only increased rapidly after the Second World War. By 1975, the end of the generation of prosperity, most Western European economies were mixed, neither capitalist nor state socialist but a hybrid that had some of the characteristics of both.

The social democrats and their allies sought to abolish poverty by a combination of redistributive taxation, national social security systems and public medical services. By extending secondary and higher education, passing anti-discrimination laws and laws about working conditions, they endeavoured to bring about equality of access and opportunity, and by all these measures, they tried to narrow the great differences in income and wealth that had existed before the war.

In 1936, before the Second World War, Keynes prophesied that the two opposed errors of pessimism, which now make so much noise in the world, will be proved wrong in our time: the pessimism of the revolutionaries who think that things are so bad that nothing can save us from violent change, and the pessimism of the reactionaries, who consider the balance of our economic and social life is so precarious that we must risk no experiments.[3]

Keynes was right, and the pessimists were confounded. During the thirty post-war years, the social democratic and liberal consensus produced a welfare state and, in most of Western Europe, planned economies; it moved towards equality of opportunity and the abolition of basic poverty. In those thirty years, there was no year in which unemployment reached the crisis levels of 10 per cent or more that were reached between the wars. There was hardly a single year in which there was not an improvement in the standard of living of the ordinary man and woman. At least in north-west Europe, primary poverty was largely abolished. For the population as a whole, there was an extension of opportunity through compulsory secondary education, through the expansion of higher education three- and fourfold, through house ownership, through an abundance of consumer goods, through the coming of television – not just a widening of opportunities but a narrowing of differences in the quality of life that had not been seen before at any stage in history.

Ralf Dahrendorf, one of the most far-seeing social thinkers of our time, said in his recent *Life Chances*, 'It is easy today to pour irony over the political syndrome which marks the climax and crisis of modernity. It is all the more important to emphasize that in many respects the social democratic consensus signifies the greatest progress which history has seen so far. Never before have so many people had so many life chances.'[4]

Dahrendorf's words have been echoed in unexpected quarters – in such an unexpected quarter, for example, as Dr Arthur Burns, Chairman of the US Federal Reserve Board from 1970 until 1978, who has remarked that 'by pre-war standards, recessions were brief and mild through the mid 1960s; both in the US and in other industrialized countries, world trade expanded rapidly under a beneficent regime of stable exchange rates; and living standards rose impressively throughout the developed world'.[5]

For thirty years, the house of Maynard Keynes stood. It was a house constructed out of names and phrases like Dumbarton Oaks and Bretton Woods, that somehow seem to sum up a sense of decency and permanency. Intended to be provisional and temporary, these international organizations and agreements set up shortly after the Second World War survived the strains and problems of the post-war decades. In the terms that were used to describe the third French Republic, they demonstrated that nothing may be so permanent as the provisional.

But the house that Keynes built has now largely been destroyed. It was weakened by the war in Vietnam and the creation on a colossal scale of the Euro-dollars needed to finance that war. It was weakened by the unwillingness of the Western powers to reconstruct the international economic institutions Keynes helped to found, the General Agreement on Tariffs and Trade, the International Monetary Fund and the World Bank, to reflect the growing influence and significance of the Third World, as newly independent countries emerged in the 1960s and 1970s. It was weakened by the refusal of the Soviet Union and her allies, for political reasons, to join these institutions. It was virtually destroyed by the failure to find a way to recycle the surpluses of the OPEC oil producers.

The tragedy is that nothing has been done to reform or extend Keynes's institutions, nor has any new structure been built on his foundations. The 1948 Marshall Plan, which helped Europe first to recover from the war and then to move on to unprecedented prosperity, has had no successor, though the gap between the needs of the Third World and the resources of the West is even wider than the gap that existed between devastated Europe and North America in 1948. The industrialized world simply flounders in the wake of those great post-war achievements.

THE POLITICAL ACHIEVEMENT

The successes of the social democratic consensus were not only economic. Marked though the economic advances were, there was also a political achievement.

In July 1945, during the course of the British general election,

Winston Churchill made a notorious broadcast in which he claimed that if the British public voted for the Labour Party, they would find that they had introduced a secret police, a Gestapo, into British domestic politics.

A similar warning was given in the USA five years later by Senator Joseph McCarthy, who saw every socialist as a communist wolf in sheep's clothing. As an overseas student at Columbia University in 1952 I was unwise enough to describe one of my fellow-students as a Marxist. The lecturer came up to me afterwards and said, 'For God's sake, never use that description again about any of your fellow-students in this seminar.' I said to him, 'Why are you getting so upset?' And he said, 'Because if you use that term about anybody in this seminar, he will never get a job.' Senator McCarthy was a latter-day witch-hunter, appealing to the hard-hats in the USA. At least that seems to me a fairly accurate description, looking back a generation. But the truth was a very different one from that enunciated by Winston Churchill or by Joseph McCarthy. The truth was that the social democratic and liberal consensus had a greater respect for democracy than any other political philosophy that preceded it or any that has come after it.

In the United Kingdom, a Labour government instituted for the first time the system of one person, one vote. It may be hard for those who are not historians to recollect this, but until 1947, it was not necessarily one person, one vote in Britain; some people had two votes or even three because they were graduates or because they had business property in a constituency other than that in which they lived.

It was a Labour government in Britain that introduced legal aid and advice in 1949, which meant that men and women were not barred from justice in the courts by their inability to pay for a decent lawyer. It was a Labour government in Britain that in 1947, by passing the Crown Proceedings Act, enabled the ordinary citizen for the first time to sue the government itself. Social democratic governments in Sweden and Norway introduced the office of the Ombudsman, later also adopted in the Federal Republic of Germany and the United Kingdom, so that individual citizens could seek redress if they believed they had suffered an injustice at the hands of a government department.

Part of the post-war achievement is the fact that since 1945 not a single country in Western Europe has been lost to democracy, apart from a short period in which Greece was under military rule. Three have come back – Spain, Portugal and Greece. Both Austria and Yugoslavia have remained outside the ambit of the great powers, being non-aligned, perhaps because both have developed new and radical economic institutions appropriate to a mixed economy.

The liberal tradition and the socialist tradition are very different, despite the fact that many of the objectives and some of the methods were common to both in the post-war period. Both words – 'liberal' and 'socialist' – suffer from the consequences of their own attractiveness. Thus a 'liberal' may be, as in the nineteenth-century Manchester tradition or in the philosophy of German liberalism, a stout upholder of free-market economics and of economic individualism; he or she may be hostile to collective provision of any kind. The word can also describe, as it does in the United States, a person whose political stance is interventionist, who favours federal and state laws against discrimination, and who can be counted on as a supporter of social services and of the consequent public expenditure. Irving Kristol described the position of many US liberals in a 1979 contribution to *Dialogue*: 'Once the liberal agendas of the 1930s, 1940s and 1950s were completed, a new agenda began to emerge, and part of American liberalism began to move left. That is, it began to move more and more towards what in Europe would be called social democracy.'[6]

THE SOCIALIST HERITAGE

Socialism, too, has been given different meanings stemming from the many roots it grew from. It is a word used equally to describe the mixed, pluralist society of Sweden and the monolithic command economies of the Soviet Union or Bulgaria. Theodore Draper, the American writer, has referred to 'the Communist usurpation of the term socialism', a term that is indeed a source of lively suspicion in the United States. Indeed, Americans, like the Russians themselves, frequently use the term 'socialist countries' to describe the Soviet bloc. For parties descended from the Marxist tradition, socialism is regarded as the penultimate stage before communism.

Communism is that stage in which, Marx said, the state would wither away – a stage that in societies that accept Marxist teaching seems stubbornly slow to come. But I will have more to say of that later.

Common to all socialist traditions is Ricardo's labour theory of value, though Ricardo himself was no socialist: that labour alone adds value, and therefore any surplus that arises after labour has been paid represents the exploitation of that labour. In so far as this is true, it is a long way from the whole truth. Anthony Crosland, that formidable latter-day exponent of democratic socialism, correctly claimed that all societies need a surplus for reinvestment if their economic capacity is to be sustained, let alone expanded. Indeed, the Soviet Union has been a prime example, raising a very substantial forced surplus from the kulaks in the 1920s and 1930s; later on, its publicly owned industries adopted pricing policies that contained large hidden tax elements. Yet Ricardo's ghost lingers on, making democratic socialists deeply uneasy about profits, even reinvested profits.

The Marxist contribution to the socialist tradition is so massive as to confound description. Its salient points, however, are well known. Economic relationships are shaped by the methods of production. Hence industrialization created an owning class, the bourgeoisie, who thrust aside the earlier landowning class, the aristocracy; and also a proletariat possessing only its own labour and exploited by the bourgeoisie. By means of revolution, the proletariat would seize the instruments of production and over-throw the ruling class. The new socialist state would be led by a dictatorship of the proletariat, accountable to the people through the revolutionary party, and governing in their interests. Then, as classes disappeared (there no longer being any function for them), the state itself would wither away, and a self-governing, non-exploitative communist society would be born, producing the world's goods and sharing them among its members 'from each according to his ability, to each according to his need'.[7] That messianic and noble vision of a society without conflict or exploitation has fired the minds of many men and women ever since – St Augustine's City of God transferred to earth as a new Jerusalem.

It is at this point that the stream of socialist tradition divides,

Ricardo, Marx and Engels all being part of the mainstream. It was Marx who said of Britain that she might conceivably move to socialism, not by revolution, but through her bourgeois Parliamentary institutions.[8] It was a remarkable thought in 1873, and it seems doubtful whether Marx had much faith in it. Other Marxists had none. Again, to quote Anthony Crosland, 'One of the errors the Marxists always made, on the basis of a faulty analysis of the nature of political conflict, was absurdly to underrate the socio-economic consequences of political democracy.'[9]

The British Labour party, begotten by a pragmatic and nonconformist trade union movement out of Marxist longings, adopted the parliamentary route, though not without misgiving. It discovered among the socio-economic consequences of political democracy, that giving the suffrage to working men made possible the creation of a constituency for redistributive taxation and greater equality, and that when the suffrage was given to women, both those working outside the home and inside it, a constituency for maternity services, health services and, in a broader sense, the welfare state was created too.

There is thus a separate strand in social democracy, commitment to the method of persuasion rather than revolution. It is not a commitment that all members of the socialist parties of Western Europe adhere to. In these broad coalitions there are segments that would support the method of revolution. The commitment to persuasion, however, is of the essence of social democracy, and distinguishes it from other heirs to the socialist tradition. The commitment, of course, was long ago transformed into a lasting relationship between democratic socialism and the electorate, a relationship that has been an important influence on the development of socialist thought. It has modified socialist doctrine because that socialist doctrine has had to be acceptable to the electorate. It has created the politics of gradualism; and it has also meant that socialism can only advance intermittently and will sometimes suffer setbacks. The great philosophic exponents of social democracy are Kautsky, Owen and Tawney; Owen and Tawney are to political thought what Vaughan Williams was to music: pastoral, gentle and humane. Tawney was quite clear about his attachment to democratic socialism. In *The Attack and Other Papers* (1953) he wrote:

'It is not certain, though it is probable, that socialism in England can be achieved by the methods proper to democracy. It is certain that it cannot be achieved by any other: nor, even if it could, should the supreme goods of civil and political liberty, in whose absence no socialist worthy of the name can breathe, be part of the price.'[10]

THE CHRISTIAN CONTRIBUTION

As ever, Tawney was marvellously farsighted. But his view about the indispensability of individual liberty was only a part of his contribution to the socialist tradition. He gave meaning to the third element in the revolutionary trinity: fraternity, the forgotten member (almost as neglected as the Holy Ghost, the third person in the Christian Trinity). The idea of fraternity Tawney saw as central to the socialist vision. For socialism is not primarily about public ownership or state control of the economy, it is about fellowship, community and participation. 'The question', he wrote in *The Attack*, 'is not merely whether the state owns and controls the means of production ... it is also who owns and controls the state.' Like Robert Owen, Tawney saw that the industrial revolution had torn apart organic feudal society and replaced the Christian concept of the whole man with the abstraction of economic man. Much of Tawney's thought is Christian in inspiration, and his socialism owes a great deal to the nonconformist tradition of brotherhood and social justice. His belief in equality grew out of the Biblical injunction that all men are brothers, that we are members one of another. 'It is absurd and degrading for men to make much of their intellectual and moral superiority to each other,' he wrote in *Equality*, 'because judged by their places in any universal scheme, they are all infinitely great or infinitely small.'[11] In 1960, Hugh Gaitskell, then the Leader of the Labour party, tried to set out the party's aims in a declaration of principle. He was at the time engaged in a major battle to alter Clause IV of the party's constitution, the clause that committed the party to the common ownership of the means of production, distribution and exchange. It is worth noting that the very first of the principles set out in Gaitskell's declaration was 'the brotherhood of man'.[12]

Christian teaching has had its effect on continental European politics also, though for many decades socialism and Christian belief were held to be incompatible, partly because of the Marxist base of much continental socialism. Christian democrats are now often described on the Continent as 'conservatives'. But the Anglo-Saxon conservative tradition is quite different from Christian democracy. Christian democracy has never been suspicious of the state, nor opposed to welfare measures in the way that American conservatives or the monetarist school in British politics are. Because the family is central to the Christian Democrat ideal, Christian parties from the late nineteenth century on favoured social benefits and family support; nor have they been opposed to public ownership. Indeed, under largely Christian Democrat governments since the war, Italy built up as extensive a public sector as did Britain under Labour governments (though several key industries in Italy were first nationalized by Mussolini). But the existence of Christian Democrat parties in Germany, Italy, Belgium and the Iberian peninsula has affected the attitude of the churches, and particularly of the Roman Catholic church, towards the social democrats. The Roman Catholic church in these countries has been ambivalent and occasionally hostile towards social democratic parties, and remains suspicious still of their Marxist roots. It has sometimes seen Christian democracy as the secular expression of Christian philosophy in the political world, a view difficult to sustain in the light of the grubby and self-seeking record of some Christian Democrat politicians. Occasionally the hierarchy has openly intervened in politics, as the German bishops did in the West German federal elections of October 1980, going well beyond their legitimate concern with moral and religious issues. Yet, paradoxically, Christian democracy and social democracy share many of the same objectives.

In the United States and Britain, there is no tradition of Christian parties, and the churches do not intervene to support one party against another, though they may press particular issues – aid for the Third World, better race relations, opposition to abortion or to euthanasia. The total separation of state education from religion in the United States has so far prevented religion from erupting into politics on the issue of education, as it has done in continental Western Europe. In Great Britain, the generous provision within the state system for denominational schools, 85 per cent of whose capital costs are met by public funds, has defused the issue completely. (In Northern Ireland, on the other hand, the segregation of schools on denominational lines has helped to keep the fuse alight, for unique and tragic historical reasons.) Abortion alone has emerged in the Anglo-Saxon countries as an explosive political question where the churches are heavily engaged. In the United States this one issue has already destroyed the careers of reputable Senators and Congressmen. But it has not brought about any commitment by the churches to a particular political party.*

The Christian contribution to democratic socialist thought is clearest in Britain, but has been highly influential in other countries too, intermingling with the contributions of Marxists, liberals, Fabians, anarchists, Chartists and many more, not forgetting the Levellers of the English Commonwealth who spoke out in the famous Putney debates: 'the poorest he that is in England hath a life to live as the greatest he', said Colonel Rainborowe.[13]

In the thirty-five years since the war, democratic socialism has been influenced by the experience of holding power and the responsibility of governing. It has evolved towards a more flexible and pragmatic philosophy. Thus in 1959 the German socialist party (SPD) at its famous Bad Godesberg conference recognized the rights of private ownership as well as the significance of public ownership. The conference committed the SPD to supporting a mixed economy. In that same year, Hugh Gaitskell failed to carry the Labour Party Conference for a similar change to Clause IV of the party's constitution. Gaitskell declared that public ownership was a means, not an end, and Labour governments since that time have adopted his approach. But the clause has become a King Charles's head, a critical symbol in the battle between Labour moderates and the Labour left.

Yet the problems of managing large-scale industry, whether publicly or privately owned, and the relations of workers to management are compelling socialists to look again at decentralized forms of control, at industrial democracy and participation,

---

* Recently the teaching of evolution in the schools has become a highly controversial issue in some states. Certain fundamentalist churches oppose any instruction in theories other than the book of Genesis.

and at the nature of the production process. The Swedish and German socialist parties have been in the vanguard in trying new approaches; so has Yugoslavia, alone among the one-party states. The Labour Party Constitution's Clause IV speaks of 'common ownership' and of 'the best obtainable system of popular administration and control of each industry or service', which is by no means the same thing as nationalization, the method largely adopted by Labour governments in Britain. Changing the decision-making structures in industry has implications far outside industry itself, on other large organizations – hospitals, schools, local government, pension funds, statutory social services. It is a difficult route back to the ideal of men and women as whole people, part of society in all its aspects, instead of men and women as economic instruments of the production process. The repercussions are incalculable. They are what some of this book is about. But before we get there, we need to look at what went wrong with welfare democracy and with the social democratic consensus, despite their remarkable achievements.

2

What Went Wrong

The political mood in the West has changed remarkably in recent years. The balance of opinion has moved against the typical product of social democratic government: government intervention in the economy, high public expenditure, the welfare state, a substantial public sector and the pursuit of equality. The intellectual winds now blow from a different quarter; the right-wing thinkers show more energy and confidence than do left-wing thinkers, many of whom reiterate tired and irrelevant dogmas or seem incapable of moving beyond their last stated position.

The conditions that between the wars bred the socialist challenge have been largely forgotten. Two generations of voters have grown up since then, and only old men and women remember the Great Depression, the pre-war dole queues and the despair out of which fascism grew. So right-wing doctrines, such as monetarism, have flourished among people innocent of their historic consequences. Now those consequences are again becoming depressingly clear, and yet another generation is learning these harsh lessons. But the new political atmosphere was not only produced by forgetfulness. It was also the product of what went wrong with socialism, both socialist theory and socialist practice. And what went wrong with socialism was not that social democratic governments failed to carry out their election pledges. Indeed, most election pledges have been loyally carried out. The trouble lay in the very pledges made, many of which failed to recognize that certain traditional objectives had been overtaken by events or found wanting in practice.

Many socialist policies have depended upon the state as their instrument; they have required an expansion in the role of central government. Socialists need to recognize the force of the antipathy that now exists towards 'big government': the multiplication of bureaucracy, the increase in cost, the feeling that government already has too large an influence over people's individual lives. Interestingly, this feeling is not directed solely against democratic socialist governments. It is an objection to big government *per se*, to government as 'big brother', or as 'a sort of unlimited liability insurance company',[1] to government interfering with everything.

At a time when Chrysler, Leyland, Rolls-Royce, Machines Bull, Pennsylvania Central and many other private firms have turned to the government to rescue them, there is felt to be a disturbing degree of dependence, both psychological and economic, on government agencies.

Socialists may dismiss public unease on this score, but they would be foolish to do so. For the resentment towards big government and its public expression, bureaucracy, is not just a resentment inspired by inefficiency. It goes much deeper than that, as the defeat of the Swedish socialist government in 1976 demonstrated – one of the most efficient governments in the Western world. It is a powerful desire to run oneself and one's own show, not to be bothered with forms and regulations, not to be treated, however rationally, as a unit rather than as a person.

The attack on 'big government' affects any political philosophy such as socialism that has government intervention as a central tenet, but the attack goes wider than that. In the United States, while big government is sometimes described as 'creeping social-ism', the real grounds of criticism are the multiplication of regula-tions, the growing involvement of the federal government in fields such as education or the rescue of private companies where previously the federal government did little or nothing, and the seeming lack of public accountability. It was this mood that helped Ronald Reagan to achieve such a striking victory. Yet, paradoxi-cally, Congress's efforts to patrol government policies and to probe in detail how federal funds have been spent produce a mirror image of 'big government' in congressional elephantiasis.

Another paradox can be seen in Britain, and no doubt in many other countries as well: the growth of administration. In 1970, the then Conservative government brought in the American industrial consultants, McKinsey & Co., to advise them on the reorganization of the National Health Service. The reorganization, in which professional interests were extensively consulted, led to a substantial increase in the number of administrative and clerical posts, and a higher proportion of administrators and clerical employees to doctors and nurses, the front line of the service.[2] Local government reorganization, under the same Conservative government, had similar consequences: more highly paid administrative posts, no evidence of improvement in local government services. Big government has its own impetus which is hard to stop, whatever the philosophy of the executive in charge. But opposition to it rubs off most on political parties identified with a substantial role for government.

THE TAXPAYERS' REVOLT

A second line of attack, clearly closely related to the reaction against 'big government', is on the high public expenditure necessitated by the welfare state. The taxpayers' revolt began in France with the Poujadist party, and was later taken up in Denmark, where Per Glijstrup's anti-tax party had a remarkable, if brief, period of success. It was an element in the 1976 defeat of the Swedish socialist government, and then reached its high-water mark in the triumphant passage of California's Proposition 13 in 1978. Proposition 13 tied local property taxes to their 1976/7 level, and imposed a 1 per cent maximum on the annual increase, effectively halving the property tax yield. But as the effects of Proposition 13 have been felt on education and other publicly financed services, public enthusiasm for tax cutting has waned. An attempt to pass a similar proposal, known as Jarvis Two, to halve California's state taxes was heavily defeated in June 1980. The recent history of anti-tax movements is one of dramatic advances which are not then sustained.

One particular form the attack on high public expenditure takes, one that is popular and easy to get across in electoral terms, is the allegation that many people are living off the welfare state who could perfectly well survive on their own. Popular newspapers on both sides of the Atlantic give a lot of space to individual cases – and there always are some – of people proclaiming how they have milked the social security system of thousands of dollars or thousands of pounds. Everybody has heard of somebody who can't be bothered to get a job, or who stays at home living on welfare because his wage in a job would be little more than his welfare cheque. The 'poverty trap' – incomes-related benefits which are lost or reduced as the breadwinner's income rises – provides a rationale for 'scrounging'. It really is true that some heads of large families may be better off not working.

Yet the evidence for large-scale 'scrounging' is thin; most people much prefer a job to enforced leisure. Nor is the popular hostility against scroungers a by-product of the welfare state. It has a much older history. Ricardo himself inveighed against the Speenhamland system, under which wages were subsidized by the parish if they fell below a minimum level which was linked to the price of bread. 'The principle of gravitation is not more certain than the tendency of such laws to change wealth and vigour into misery and weakness', Ricardo wrote in *On the Principles of Political Economy and Taxation* (1817). It might be Professor Milton Friedman speaking. At the end of the eighteenth century, that indefatigable Utilitarian Jeremy Bentham turned his mind to the rehabilitation of convicts, many of them indigent people without work. He proposed to establish a panopticon, a sort of multi-industry establishment, which he described, chillingly, as 'a mill to grind rogues honest, and idle men industrious'.[3] Similar wishes are still expressed on the floor of Congress or the House of Commons by ardent Conservatives; only the language alters.

The consequence of big government and high public expenditure is inflation, say the critics of the social democratic consensus. Unquestionably, inflation was a much more significant feature of industrialized economies in the 1970s than in the 1950s or 1960s, and it has persisted even at times of mild recession. In the period from 1958 to 1964, United States wholesale prices, for example, rose by an average of 1 per cent per annum. In the period between 1964 and 1968, US wholesale prices rose annually by an average of 2 per cent. Between 1972 and 1978, US wholesale prices rose by an average of 10 per cent a year.

Many people put inflation down to profligate public spending, to the creation of money, to over-full employment and to the welfare state. But whatever the reason they give, one thing is clear: it is no longer true that inflation and recession cannot exist side by side. The two are now compatible; the stagflation economy has combined alternatives that Keynesians believed could not be combined.

There are other factors that have influenced the change in the political mood. Social democrats in Western Europe and their liberal allies in North America have either governed or shared in government for much of the past thirty-five years. They have become part of the governing establishment and therefore they bear responsibility for what has actually happened. Two bodies of political opinion have been thereby alienated from them. The first resents the decline of Western power, especially that of the old British and French empires and subsequently of the United States. It holds Western governments responsible for this decline, declaring that they have been pusillanimous, indecisive, weak and lacking in conviction. The conciliatory positions adopted by social democrat and liberal governments towards independence movements in the Third World and the attempts to reach agreement on disarmament and détente are condemned as the selling-out of Western interests.

Once one is persuaded that individual governments can fundamentally alter historic trends such as the break-up of empire, then it is easy to make the jump to regarding the social democratic/liberal consensus as a form of betrayal. While only a small minority on the right take so extreme a view, much larger sections of public opinion are uneasy about the rapid relative decline in Western economic and political power, which seems to be accelerating. Many in the older generation have been brought up on myths of national greatness and even of racial superiority, which make any explanation other than the failure of government hard to accept. In the United States, Richard Nixon and later Ronald Reagan both exploited this sense of anger and frustration.

REVOLUTIONARIES AND REFORMERS

The second body of opinion is very different. It is made up of Utopians, purists and revolutionaries who prefer their socialism untrammelled by the responsibilities of government. In his biography of Hugh Gaitskell, Philip Williams described the struggle in the Labour party: 'Labour's crisis in the 1960s was a conflict about its character – whether the party was to be a protest movement or a prospective government of the country.'[4] The struggle has always been like this, because socialist parties include those who want to reform society, recognizing the limitations imposed by representative democracy, those who want to overthrow the existing system and put something new in its place, and those who simply want to dream of an unattainable ideal. For these last, Master Olaf spoke in Strindberg's play *The Father* (1887): 'It wasn't victory I wanted: it was the battle!' Socialist governments could never fulfil the impossible requirements of the Utopians, and it is doubtful whether the Utopians actually want them to. But those who want to overthrow rather than reform the existing political and economic system are serious in their intentions, and deserve to be taken seriously.

The conflict between the protesters and the potential governors in democratic socialist parties is usually characterized as the conflict between left and right. Yet this description will not do. There can be advocates of very radical policies among the potential governors, their radicalism tempered only by the constraints of getting the policy accepted and making it operate. There can be protesters whose main protest is against change, especially change that adversely affects their vested interests. The gulf lies between those who want policies that can be carried out, and carried out within the existing political system, and those who believe that the existing political system must be broken first.

Here lies the nub of the old argument – for the old argument between revolutionaries and reformers precedes both in time and in logic the argument between those who want a movement of protest and those who want a prospective government. The reformers want to modify the present political system in many ways, but ultimately it is the political system they prefer above all others: pluralist, respectful of minorities, based on individual opinion and individual conscience. Furthermore, the reformers cannot divorce the political system of pluralist democracy from a pluralist economic system, a mixed economy. Politics and economics are interdependent. A

pluralist democracy complements a pluralist economy; a monolithic political system complements monolithic economic ownership
and control.

The revolutionaries want to break the pluralist or mixed
economic system, and hence (whatever they may say) the pluralist
political system which emanates from it. The two cannot be
disconnected. So the revolutionaries would ultimately be bound to
destroy pluralist democracy. The democracy they believe in is
something very different, democratic centralism or what Lenin
called inner-party democracy. Argument takes place within the
ruling party. Once the decision is made, the argument ends, and all
party cadres are bound by it. It is thus imposed through the party's
organizational structure on all the institutions in which the party is
predominant, from the legislature or the parliamentary party to the
workshop committee. Stalin inveighed against the whole concept of
parliamentary representatives independent of the party in his book
on Leninism:

> The opportunist theory of the 'independence' and 'neutrality' of non-
> party organizations, which theory is the progenitor of independent
> parliamentarians and publicists who are isolated from the Party, and of
> narrow-minded trade unionists and cooperative society officials who have
> become petty bourgeois, is wholly incompatible with the theory and
> practice of Leninism.[5]

There is no possibility of reconciling the reformers and the
revolutionaries, for their objectives are incompatible. Reformers
some times represent themselves as cautious revolutionaries. 'Yes,'
they say, 'we are moving along the same path as you, only more
slowly. We must persuade people to support us. We must win
elections. So we mustn't frighten people away.'

But reformers are not cautious revolutionaries. Theirs is a
different political tradition. Reformers would never want to see
pluralist democracy destroyed, even if a majority voted so to do.
Reformers cannot support the concentration of power inherent in a
monolithic economy, whether it is commanded by a corporatist,
communist or military government. Sparta and Moscow are
equally abhorrent to them. So the truth is that the goals of reformers
and revolutionaries are different, and always have been. The

common objectives of greater equality and the abolition of poverty cannot bridge the philosophic divide. And what is happening to socialist parties is that that divide has become explicitly – as implicitly it always was – unbridgeable.

Socialist governments, trying to hide from themselves this unbridgeable philosophic divide, have concentrated on the goals the reformers share with the revolutionaries, equality and the abolition of poverty. Yet even these have proved unexpectedly elusive. Post-war governments, not all socialist ones, made important advances through universal secondary education, the massive expansion of higher education, the introduction of publicly financed health services, much better retirement pensions and earnings-related sickness and unemployment benefits. As I said in Chapter 1, opportunities were widened and differences in the quality of life narrowed beyond anything ever seen before. But the roots of inequality lie very deep, back even before birth. A child's health is affected by whether or not its mother has had adequate pre- and postnatal care, by her nutrition and by its infant environment. A child's capacity to learn is affected by its surroundings, by the amount of interest shown by its parents, by the accommodation in which they live, not least by the expectations society has of him or her. Socialists discovered that the major improvements made in health, education and social services raised everybody's standards, but did not greatly narrow the differentials between income or occupational groups. Thus infant mortality in Britain fell and the expectation of life rose after the introduction of mother-and-child clinics during the war, followed in 1948 by a National Health Service free at the point of need. But still large differences persisted between regions and between social groups. A 1980 survey, thirty years after the introduction of the National Health Service, found that twice as many babies of unskilled or semi-skilled manual workers died before they reached the age of one month, as did the babies of professional and executive parents.[6] Secondary education for all, the trebling of higher education places and an extensive system of student grants enabled many thousands more working-class youngsters to go to university: yet the proportion of university students from manual workers' homes remained stubbornly unaltered at about 25 per cent of the total. One part of the explanation is that employment structures changed; more people absolutely and relatively are today employed in professional and white-collar occupations and fewer in blue-collar jobs than thirty years ago. Another part of the explanation is the extraordinary ability of the middle classes to get most out of public services, by a combination of know-how, self-confidence, persistence and articulacy.

POVERTY

The welfare state and the publicly financed health services largely eliminated crude primary poverty. Arguments demonstrating that more people are poor than ten or twenty years ago are deceptive because they leave out of account changes in the definition of poverty. Poverty before the war meant having no possessions beyond the barest necessities. Nowadays, families owning a reasonably furnished house or even a car may be defined as poor; for example in Britain they may qualify for what is known as supplementary benefit. Because the general standard of living has risen a great deal, the level at which people are defined as poor has been raised too, and rightly so. There is an irony in the fact that any government that raises the level at which people may qualify for supplementary benefit immediately 'creates' more poor people. It makes a rod for its own back.

Definition apart, however, poverty is now growing again. More people in the early 1980s are unemployed, and more are unemployed for longer. Social changes have led to more broken marriages; households headed by single mothers constitute the poorest large section of the population. Retired people, the other large group that is relatively poor, are living longer; as they become too old to do part-time work, as their savings run out and their physical dependency increases, they become poorer still. The paradox of the welfare state is that it has sustained those who make the greatest demands upon it. Thus publicly financed health services have saved thousands of severely handicapped babies who once would have died at birth, and have prolonged the lives of ailing elderly people, whose need for medical attention far exceeds that of the working population.

The social democrats were slow in getting to grips with these inherent contradictions. When Aneurin Bevan launched the National Health Service in 1948, he believed that its need for resources would actually diminish as the backlog of ill-health was dealt with. In one respect, he was right: vaccinations, immunization and other preventive public health measures have eliminated or vastly reduced the risk from many diseases, such as tuberculosis and diphtheria, at very low cost. But these large savings have been more than offset by the health service's expensive success in prolonging life, to which must be added the frightening costs of the drugs and equipment required by many of the new intensive medical techniques.

The opponents of the welfare state have tried to contain the high public expenditure that is its necessary concomitant, and are seeking to cut it back. Already the consequences are becoming clear, not only in growing numbers of people in poverty, but also in widening income, opportunity and wealth differentials. The welfare state has been a crucial element in maintaining the political stability of the Western world in the turbulent post-war years. The very conservative forces which deprive it of resources may come to regret the consequences of their actions. Unemployed people are being forced back into poverty by the removal of earnings-related unemployment pay and the breaking of the links between benefits and the cost of living. Ethnic minorities and the inhabitants of run-down inner cities see a bleak future with little hope of a good job or an improved environment. It is likely that these men and women will become a volatile and disaffected political force. The welfare state has brought both prosperity and stability to the industrialized countries and to Western Europe in particular. Government intervention and government action have also improved the quality of life for many people, ranging from the subsidization of railways to the funding of education. Without central government funds and central government action, the discrepancies between rich and poor regions, between people in different occupations and people of different racial origins would be much wider than they are. No socialist can advocate weak government or the undermining of the welfare state. The issues for socialists are different ones. Can some of the powers of central government be devolved downwards, to regional authorities or even to local communities? Can the welfare state be made less bureaucratic, and can it involve its own 'clients', the public it serves, in providing social services as well as in accepting them? Political parties, and in particular socialist parties, advocate big government in order to overcome inequality. The electors then react against being over-taxed and over-governed. Only by greater participation and by decentralization whenever it is compatible with social justice can we begin to resolve this conflict.

COMMUNISM'S FAILURE

I cannot end any chapter on what seems to have gone wrong for socialism without referring to the most negative influence of all, the failure of the Communist revolution. I have already pointed out that the socialist tradition came to a fork in the road; part of it developed as democratic socialism, part as Marxist-Leninism. Because there were elements in the tradition common to both, the failure of the one was bound to colour attitudes towards the other. The social democratic Abel has done well by the people; not so the Communist Cain. But they were sons in the same family.

In 1935, Sidney and Beatrice Webb, those distinguished Fabians, wrote a book called *Soviet Communism: a New Civilization?* Two years later they removed the question mark because it was so obvious to them and to their colleagues of the left that the Soviet Union was, indeed, a new civilization.

In the forty years since then, the reality of the Communist experience has been gradually and painfully revealed. There was the forced collectivization of agriculture in the 1930s. But that could be explained: the new Soviet state, surrounded by enemies, had to produce a surplus for industrial investment, and agriculture was by far the largest sector of the economy from which that surplus had to come. With hindsight, it is highly questionable whether collectivization produced a quicker or larger surplus than land reform and taxation would have done. What is certain is that in the process millions of peasant farmers were killed.

Then there were the Moscow trials, when Stalin purged the party and the army of his rivals and enemies, many of them devoted Bolsheviks who had fought valiantly for the Revolution. There was, also, the attempted destruction of the ethnic minorities, such as the Tartars, partly by forced exile, partly by elimination.

After the war came the colonization of Eastern Europe, connived at by the Western allies. Weakened by war and ravaged by Nazi occupation, many Eastern European countries welcomed the Russians to whom they later succumbed. I met some of the sad and amazed straggle of refugees who came across the Czech-Bavarian border in 1948, among them committed social democrats brought up in the great tradition of Masaryk and Beneš. The Western allied soldiers occupying Germany forced many of these brave men and women back across the frontier to almost certain death or imprisonment.

The Czechs in 1948 provided only the first of the encounters between the Soviet Union and the peoples of Eastern Europe. The industrial workers of East Germany rebelled in 1953, the workers and intellectuals of Hungary in the autumn of 1956 when Britain and France were engaged in their mendacious invasion of Egypt. Czechoslovakia's second brave experiment, Dubček's 'socialism with a human face', was destroyed by Russian tanks in August 1968. Since then, Eastern Europe has simmered, sometimes near the brink of explosion like Poland in 1977 and again after the mass strikes of Gdansk and Szczecin in 1980. Russian army tanks have rumbled into Afghanistan, that rebellious outpost of so many imperialisms, of which the USSR is only the most recent.

Even within the USSR herself, the revolution is a travesty. As Milovan Djilas pointed out in *The New Class*,[7] within the Soviet bloc a new ruling class has been created, more powerful, more difficult to reform, harder to change than was the old ruling class of aristocrats and landowners. The bureaucrats of the monolithic state have become privileged, unaccountable and self-perpetuating.

I remember my own experience in the 1960s when I was serving as a minister of state in Harold Wilson's government. I went to Moscow in September 1969, flying economy, and as I came down the ladder I noticed, through a half-open eye, a line-up of officers and other top brass beside the first-class steps. I took no further notice and went into the terminal building. Half an hour later, a somewhat confused group of top brass and military men came into the terminal to ask what had happened to the British minister they were intending to meet. It was inconceivable that somebody who was a member of a government would travel as an ordinary citizen. So far had the new class taken on the pattern of the old. In 1980, one of the demands of the independent Polish trade union, Solidarity, was that bureaucrats should cease to have special privileges, such as access to shops with imported goods not available to ordinary citizens.

Sakharov and others have told us about the repression of unorthodoxy and the intellectual strait-jacket in which the Soviet Union's intellectuals have to operate. Solzhenitsyn has testified to the systematic repression of religious and political dissidents which he described in his volumes on *The Gulag Archipelago*,[8] a more efficient and thorough-going development of the labour camps of the Tsar.

So strong was the Communist ideal, so large did it loom in the politics of the 1920s and 1930s, that when the dream exploded it left behind a whole assortment of political fragments, highly radio-active and with long half-lives, that socialists still have to respond to. Among these fragments is Euro-Communism.

In April 1980, a conference of European Communist parties was held in Bucharest in order to discuss 'Peace and Disarmament'. The Yugoslav party decided to join the Spaniards and the Italians in refusing to attend, because they were unwilling to be used as a cover for the Soviet invasion of Afghanistan. It was only one example of many such. The Communist movement is now deeply split, to the point where the divisions resemble the great schisms in the Christian church of the fourteenth century. There is the rift between its leading members, the Soviet Union and China. There are the various heretical movements in Eastern Europe. Even within the Communist cadres of Western Europe who have freely chosen to belong, the parties of Spain, Italy, Yugoslavia and, on occasion, the British and French, have differed profoundly from the CPSU (the Communist Party of the Soviet Union) on such matters as human rights, civil liberties, détente, the dictatorship of the proletariat and the value of representative 'bourgeois' democracy. Euro-Communism in some form is likely to have a long half-life. There are other fragments: the Utopians of the left have gone from the Soviet Union to China, from China to Cuba, from Cuba to Israel's kibbutzes, from Israel to Tanzania, restlessly trying to find some real-life example of the ideal they want to achieve. And there are the revolutionary romantics and Trotskyites, wedded to an ideal of politics which has never been attained anywhere, but which, in theory, might one day be achieved if only revolution could in some way be harnessed to the perfectibility of imperfect human beings.

Last but not least, there have been anarchy and nihilism, those extreme forms of rejection of society. Their recruits are often the children of rich and privileged members of society, uneasy with their wealth and bitter about the comfortable conformity of Western bourgeois society. Reform is too slow for them, and revolution too uncertain. So the anarchists and nihilists choose destruction for its own sake. If they know what they will put in its place, they do not tell us. Their objectives are as futile as the technological destruction loosed on Vietnam or Afghanistan by the great industrialized powers; they are its alter ego. Ralf Dahrendorf quotes a pathetic scrawl written on a wall in Lisbon at the time of the revolution in Portugal, 'Anarchy, yes, but not too much.'[9]

Social democrats have not entirely avoided the fall-out from the Communist experiment's collapse. But one essential difference between social democrats and Communists is that social democrats never swallowed the millennialism that was implicit in Marx. They took much else from Marx. They took the concept of the labour theory of value as he developed it from its origins in Ricardo. They took the concept of a class structure based on the production system. But always somewhere deep inside themselves they recognized that a political and economic system cannot overnight alter the human beings that work within it. Perhaps implicitly they subscribed to Immanuel Kant's (1724–1804) warning, 'Out of the crooked timber of humanity, no straight thing can ever be made.'[10]

The tragedy of the Communist experiment is that it failed to recognize that power does indeed corrupt, even power wrested by a workers' revolution from an old ruling class. It is an experiment that achieved a great deal: industrialization, universal education, good social services, an infrastructure of public services unknown before. But all this has been overwhelmed by the privilege, brutality and corruption of the system of government. Lenin warned against Stalin succeeding him, but it was too late; the system had grown beyond him. The revolution, it was said of France in 1789, eats its own children. Stalin became the devourer. Nor is it any excuse to say that Stalin was mad. The system could not get rid of him. Any system of government that makes no provision for succession, choice and the effective accountability of the rulers to the people will rot from within, however noble its initial ideals. That is why Tawney was right to say that socialism without liberty is not worth having.

In the aftermath of the Communist failure and the reaction against socialist ideals, three new and confident actors have come on to the political stage. Two of them have tried their hands before in slightly different costumes.

The first is the new conservatism, an old orthodoxy decked out in the current fashion of monetarism. The second is political extremism. We have met him before, brown-shirted in the great stadium at Olympia in 1936, drunk on words in the Bierkellers of Munich in 1934, goosestepping in East Berlin every post-war Mayday. Looking at him, and at his urbane conservative companion, we wonder if each generation in the audience has to relearn by painful experience the mistakes of its parents, or even of its grandparents.

The other actor is a tyro, inexperienced and rather confused. But he's interesting, because he has some new lines. He embodies the new romanticism compounded of concern for the environment, love of small communities, suspicion of centralization and bureaucracy; he has flowers in his hair.

3

The Challengers

The new romanticism mentioned at the end of the last chapter is to be found in the 'green parties' that are nowadays challenging the traditional parties in Western Europe. It appears in the United States in ecological groups, in organizations favouring new community-based life-styles and among those who believe that the economic system should be fundamentally altered in a way that makes it quite different from what it is today, essentially by moving towards a much more decentralized society.

The new romanticism appeals to socialists because it is concerned less with profitable production than with the quality of life. Its followers believe that a better quality of life can be shared by everybody, however humble or however poor. It also appeals to socialists because implicit within it is the idea that men and women should not be *subjected* to an economic system, but rather should *dominate* it. The new romantics believe that the economic system known as industrialism – and they would not distinguish between private capitalism and state capitalism – has destroyed organic communities and dehumanized those who work within it. They would have no difficulty in agreeing with Robert Owen that 'the general diffusion of manufactures throughout a society generates a new character in its inhabitants, and as this character is formed upon a principle quite unfavourable to individual or general happiness, it will produce most lamentable and permanent ends ...',[1] though they might not all agree with Owen's prescription of legislative interference and direction as the countervailing force. They would enthusiastically endorse Karl Polanyi's account of the nineteenth century in that underestimated masterpiece, *The Great Transformation*: 'The conflict between the market and the elementary requirements of an organized social life provided the century with its dynamics, and produced the typical strains and stresses which ultimately destroyed that society.'[2]

The new romanticism was born of a dislike of the impersonality of technology, of resistance to bureaucracy and the destruction of small communities, and of fears about the economic pressures on the earth itself. Phrases like 'plant earth' or 'spaceship earth', to describe the fragile ecology on which we all depend, spring readily to the lips of the new romantics. They might take as their political slogan one that was put up during the period of the abortive student revolution in Paris in 1968, '*L' imagination au pouvoir*' – something that may be a little too much to hope for from politics as we know it.

The new romantics reject the conventional projection for the future. That future, as seen by conservatives and socialists alike, is to be more economic growth, more effort to compete with others for limited resources of energy and raw materials, more emphasis on efficiency, productivity and marketing; but such a future, in the eyes of the romantics, would run up against the finite capacity of the earth to produce fossil fuels, minerals, clean air and water as known resources are plundered. Furthermore, the new romantics recognize that there are indeed social limits to growth, as Fred Hirsch maintained in his stimulating book of that name.[3] New cars, Hirsch pointed out, fill the roads, yet there is no pleasure in sitting in a queue of acrid car exhausts on a Sunday afternoon. Tranquil beauty spots fill up with tourists, and their tranquillity and beauty are both destroyed. The clear seas become polluted by human and industrial waste, so no one can swim in them. All these things have happened.

One of the finest expressions of this element of romanticism was by the modern poet, Philip Larkin, in a poem about England called 'Going, going':

> it seems just now
> To be happening so very fast;
> Despite all the land left free.
> For the first time I feel somehow
> That it isn't going to last,

That before I snuff it, the whole
Boiling will be bricked in
Except for the tourist parts –
First slum of Europe: a role
it won't be so hard to win,
With a cast of crooks and tarts.

And that will be England gone,
The shadows, the meadows, the lanes,
The guildhalls, the carved choirs.
There'll be books; it will linger on
In galleries; but all that remains
For us will be concrete and tyres.[4]

That feeling runs very deep. It was put in a more philosophic form by Ralf Dahrendorf in *Life Chances*; 'Life chances', he said, 'are a function of two elements: options and ligatures.'[5] Options are opportunities, the choices each of us has. Ligatures are allegiances or linkages. Dahrendorf pointed to the sense in which the quality of life, as distinct from the quantity of production, is related to these ligatures or linkages, to the relationships that people have with their community, with their family, with the history of their particular neighbourhood, with their ability to find around them familiar things. It is these things, not only opportunities or choices, that spell out our identity and give meaning to our lives.

The quality of life, therefore, is made not only out of a widening of opportunities, but also out of a sense of belonging, of being cared for, of being wanted, of being part of a network of relationships with people and also with objects.

The new romanticism, in my view, has got something to offer to the traditional political parties that they would be unwise to reject or to fail to recognize. Ligatures and linkages matter, as well as opportunities and options. One thing the new politics is about is how far socialists can understand the significance of the quality of life, of ligatures and linkages, as well as the significance of wider opportunities and choices often derived from economic growth. They should understand – for ligatures are what fellowship and fraternity are all about.

THE NEW CONSERVATIVES

The other new actor on the political stage is the new – or, better, the retread – conservatism. The new conservatism is extremely confident, and expresses itself in ways that suggest there can be no serious criticism, no real objection to the arguments that it puts forward.

In addition to the new conservatives' confidence, there is the simplicity of their doctrine. Nobody should underestimate the power of simplicity in politics. If a politician comes up with a simple formula, for example that the supply of money directly relates to the level of inflation, then many people in a democracy will feel that that politician has managed to find the answer to the problems that beset them, and they will be grateful to him or her that it should be so.

The new conservatism is also remarkably bold. It puts forward simple, clear policies, and it claims that those policies will meet the problems that disturb and worry people at the present time. If I may take the high apostle himself, Professor Milton Friedman claims that consumers are protected by the market and that it is in the nature of free markets to produce the best product at the lowest price. Professor Friedman expounds the merits of the market economy, its flexibility, its competitivity, its sensitivity to consumer demand. He has a point, for after a generation of command economies and planned economies, economists and consumers are much more conscious than they used to be of the limitations of state control. The market matches demand and supply better than planners do. It responds more easily to changing fashion and new needs. It is rather good at getting rid of unsuccessful enterprises and at sorting out the successes from the failures. It has the advantage of being a highly decentralized form of decision making.

THE FREE MARKET

Professor Friedman, however, overstates his case – often to a ludicrous extent. There are many needs the market is incapable of meeting, because they are collective needs – for clean water, clean air, public health, a good transport system. The market is geared to individual demands and to individual purses; in meeting them, it does not count social costs or social consequences. Furthermore, there are individual demands that cannot be made effective because the individual cannot afford to satisfy them: typically, treatment for serious illness, chronic invalidism, care in old age. The market is a mechanism ill-adapted to the cycles of an individual's life history, which move from dependence through independence back to dependence again, and also to the cycles of the economy. In his recent book *Free to Choose*, Professor Friedman asserts: 'Sooner or later, and perhaps sooner than many of us expect, ever bigger governments will destroy both the prosperity that we care for in the free market and even the human freedom proclaimed so eloquently in the Declaration of Independence.'[6] In an obvious sense, the Professor must be right. Total government, controlling the whole economy, would indeed be likely to destroy both prosperity and human freedom. But again his case is hopelessly overstated. In many European countries public expenditure constitutes 40 per cent or more of the gross national product. Yet who is to say that Sweden or Denmark or the Federal Republic of Germany are less prosperous and less free than Spain, Argentina or Brazil, in which a much smaller proportion of the gross national product goes into public expenditure? Indeed the extremes of income and wealth characteristic of societies dominated by free market capitalism are not conducive to human freedom or to democratic political systems. Men and women without access to decent working conditions, education, housing and health do not fully share in their society. They are not accorded the human dignity that is intrinsic to the democratic process. Their opportunities and their choices are crippled by the unequal distribution of resources. Even if such a country has some form of election, ostensibly based on a universal and secret franchise, the great disparities in economic power will influence the many who are weak to bow to the wishes of the few who are strong.

MONETARISM

But there is, I think, an even more fundamental objection to monetarism. The essence of monetarism is the belief that control over the quantity of money is the key to control of inflation. Certainly control over the supply of money will have a quite rapid impact on a competitive free market economy, by way of prices, wages, earnings and so forth. But as Robert Leknehman put it in a *Commentary* symposium, 'There seems to be an embarrassing shortage of the free markets cherished by their adherents.'[7] The markets of Western industrialized economies are not characterized by anything like perfect competition but rather by competitive imperfections. Many industries are dominated by one or a few companies, which effectively influence price structures. They can limit or even destroy competition by the use of such mechanisms as loss leaders or discounts. They can buy up patents or license new inventions so as to deny them to their competitors. Big companies may be able to use powerful purchasing positions to bargain for a lower price for the goods they buy in, whether these are raw materials, energy or components. Furthermore, companies with established or dominant market positions can obtain finance at favourable rates, while small companies or new competitors often pay heavily for loans or credit. In a tight money market these latter may be unable to obtain capital funds at all.

The expensive and sophisticated technologies of advanced industrial society present further obstacles to truly competitive markets. In such industries as oil refining, newspaper printing or chemicals, the threshold cost of setting up a new firm is colossal; only firms with vast resources behind them can attempt entry into the field. Furthermore, where technologies are advancing fast, as with the design of machine tools in engineering, the cost of replacement may become prohibitive. A firm that could have afforded to tool up a workshop or a small engineering factory in the 1950s will find that up-to-date machinery is faster, more efficient and more sophisticated. But the capital cost of this new equipment is likely to be much higher in real terms, and the cost of maintaining sophisticated plant is often more expensive too. So a business may be overwhelmed by this factor alone, even though its order books are healthy and its production costs competitive. Advanced technologies do not favour small- and medium-sized firms; at least, they have not done so up to now, though the situation is changing.

The building of brand loyalties by advertising and special offers is another factor unfavourable to would-be competitors. Advertising is an ambivalent ally of competitive markets; it provides information to consumers, but it also creates loyalties that may be irrational, and may make it difficult for a product actually offering better value to compete.

The growing interaction between government and private industry also weights the balance in favour of large well-established firms against small companies and newcomers. In the bargaining about laws, regulations, environmental protection and taxation in all its many forms, governments consult industry and above all they consult big industry. In Western Europe, where methods of consultation have become formalized so that they almost invariably involve 'the social partners', the employer or management partner is usually the association of big businesses – the CBI in Britain or the German Employers' Confederation. Those outside can have little effect on the outcome, yet the outcome may profoundly affect them. In the United States, professionally organized lobbies can have a significant impact on congressional reactions to the executive's policy proposals, and indeed on the proposals themselves. The power of the lobbies inevitably reflects the power of those who pay for them, the big battalions.

The same pattern of economic domination and political power characterizes Western labour markets. Powerful trade unions can, in certain industries, control recruitment and redundancy. They can determine how many people shall be trained, and they can define the qualifications they will recognize for the attainment of skilled status – often including the passage of time. In industries crucial to the modern production process, such as electricity generation or oil refining or tanker driving, unions can protect their members against the impact of tight money on wages; the cost of labour in these industries is insignificant compared to the cost of losing output. Indeed, so interdependent is the modern industrial system that certain groups of workers have almost total power over it; they can literally determine whether the whole machine grinds to a halt.

Trade unions also operate within the polity. They too, like industry, consult, lobby and push for what they want. Their influence on minimum wage legislation, conditions of work, the inflow and outlow of labour, can be profound. And again, as with industry, it is the big battalions – and the strategically placed unions – that count.

Such influences, constraints and institutional rigidities sit uneasily with monetary theory. As John Pinder has said,

The monetarist doctrine, or any other policy confined to the management of global demand, assumes that the markets for products and for factors of production are nearly enough perfect to generate satisfactory employment and production once the money supply or the global demand is right. My diagnosis is that markets are now imperfect enough to generate either high unemployment or high inflation or both, whatever the money supply or the level of demand.[8]

Thus tight control of the money supply in an imperfect economy hits investment and employment harder and sooner than it hits inflation. When interest rates increase, firms put off new investment; vulnerable firms unable to finance working capital go to the wall; moreover, higher costs are often passed on in the form of higher prices, certainly where a firm dominates pricing structures. (Incidentally my experience as Prices Minister taught me to what a great extent prices are 'administered' in Britain, that is to say set by firms, not by the market. It also taught me how effectively inconvenient competition can be destroyed, especially by the judicious use of discounts, bulk pricing and loss leaders.)

DESTROYING JOBS

Tight money, similarly, hits jobs long before it hits wages. Organized labour is often strong enough to resist and delay any attempt to drive real wages down; it has been strengthened in Britain and other Western European countries by laws protecting employees against unfair dismissal and obliging firms to contribute to substantial redundancy payments usually based on length of service. So employers will take the easiest way out if they are financially under pressure. They will cease recruiting, lay off their newest or least well organized employees, and only very reluctantly, if at all, stand up to the full might of unions engaged in collective bargaining. Of course this must be qualified in the American situation, where less than 25 per cent of the workforce is in trade unions, and where workers are much more likely to be organized in the traditional and declining industries of the north-east and the middle west than in the new industries of the Sunbelt (the south and the south-west). There tight money may indeed lower wages before it reduces employment; but that is not true where trade unions are strong. Real wages will only fall when unemployment has gone so high that it has seriously undermined the unions' bargaining power.

In a BBC lecture in 1980, Professor Friedman himself went some way to concede that monetarism works in a mysterious way its wonders to perform. 'Reduced monetary growth', he said, 'produces a subsequent slowdown in spending, reflected first in output and employment and later in inflation.' Indeed, if one tries to impose the new conservatism at the macroeconomic level without dealing in any way with the microeconomic structure – the institutions and structures of power, influence and control in our economies – the net effect is that macroeconomic policies are visited upon the social and political fabric via mass unemployment and mass bankruptcy before they actually begin to operate on inflation. In Britain, where there has been a very substantial shift towards retread conservatism, political and social structures may break down and large parts of industry be destroyed before the economic results that are supposed to flow from these draconian policies are actually reached. By the time monetarism has 'saved' the British economy, there may be no economy left to save.

The monetarist landscape reminds me of a river pouring into innumerable small streams and channels in an estuary. In spate, the river fills all the streams and channels; at times of drought, each need accommodate only a trickle. But the real economic landscape is one in which streams have been dammed and blocked off; channels have been fitted with locks and pumps. So the river water, the money supply, forced into certain directions and excluded from others, impacts on the unprotected areas as flood or drought. Those without jobs cannot get them, while those with jobs are at least to some extent protected; new firms seeking access to capital are excluded, while those that are well-established can still be accommodated.

Far from being fair, competition in such circumstances is

distorted, and the word itself loses meaning. Because the impact of monetary policy is so uneven, it can strain the political fabric to the point at which it tears. Imperfect markets cannot be smashed to bits by such overarching theories. They can be tackled only by combining structural microeconomic policies with the general direction laid down in macroeconomic policies. Economic theory owes – though it often fails to pay – recognition and respect to political and social realities. As the recent report[9] of the Brandt Commission pointed out, the rigorous pursuit of conservative financial policies can be very serious for developing countries. It may put democratic institutions themselves at risk.

THE DOMINATION OF ECONOMICS

The challenge to the social democratic and liberal consensus comes both from the left – the state socialists – and from the new conservatism. There is indeed a curious affinity between them. This affinity is based upon their common belief that the economic system should subject the human being to its own requirements, to economic laws. I believe, to the contrary, that at a certain level of sufficiency, which has been achieved in the Western world, the economic system and economic laws should be subject to the requirements of the whole human being, not only to his economic needs.

Monetarism, for all its limitations, has filled the intellectual vacuum in conservative thought. Many of us may feel its influence arises from the maturing of a new generation of conservatives whose folk memories of the depression years have faded or even vanished. In politics, so often, each generation repeats the mistakes of its grandparents. So we retreat not to yesterday, but to the day before yesterday. Nevertheless, conservatism has the wind in its sails. The liberals, the progressives, the social democrats, have exhausted the conventional thinking of the post-war years. The social democratic consensus was based above all on constant economic growth. The pursuit of equality and of social justice was immensely eased by that growth; in President Kennedy's words, 'A rising tide lifts all ships.' But the growth, like the political and economic theories based upon it, is now no longer sure, no longer predictable. Where does social democracy go from here? Can it surmount its own sudden decline in confidence, and confront the attacks that are levelled against it from both the far left and the newly resurgent right? Can it put forward policies and theories that are based upon the total human being, not just economic man, but economic, political, and for that matter, cultural and spiritual man?

In the words of Tawney, 'These are times which are not ordinary and in such times it is not enough to follow the road. It is necessary to know where it leads and if it leads nowhere, to follow another.'[10]

The road that was pursued by state socialism and, for other reasons, the road that is being pursued now by the new conservatism lead to societies we do not want to live in. Therefore, what we ought to consider is whether we should follow another road, and where it might take us.

4

How The World Has Changed

The outstanding achievement of post-war democratic governments was the steady improvement in the standard of living of ordinary people. That improvement depended upon economic growth, which in turn was based on cheap resources of energy, raw materials and food. Today resources are no longer cheap. Economic growth is no longer certain. The improvement in the standard of living in most countries has ceased. For some, particularly the unemployed, the standard of living has declined dramatically.

Projections for the economic growth of the West in the first half of the 1980s make depressing reading. Of course these projections reflect the current recession, the most serious since before the war. But there is reason to believe that what is going on is not just a pause in a long upward cycle, but a deeper and more lasting change. If so, social and economic policies based on the expectation of rapid economic growth will have to be revised. Redistribution of wealth and income becomes much more difficult if the gross national product is constant or in decline. Public expenditure then has to compete for a larger share of a stable, or even declining, national product. Without growth, the redistributive policies of democratic socialism inevitably make demands upon the existing material standards of the better-off sections of the population. So let me begin by analysing the prospects for growth in the future, based upon the changes that have taken and are taking place.

THE ENERGY CRISIS

When the British Chancellor of the Exchequer, Sir Geoffrey Howe, decided in his budget of April 1980 to increase the price of oil by twenty pence a gallon, there was only a distant creak, the sound of some very vague but already abandoned protest among the British population. Western Europe, unlike the USA, gave up a long time ago the hope that there would ever again be low oil prices. That is one element in our assumptions about the world we live in that has drastically changed. Most of us know that the price of oil has gone up sixteenfold in money terms since 1973. All of us know that the West's degree of dependence on the highly unstable region of the Middle East has increased greatly over recent years. In the case of the United States, oil imports nearly doubled between 1974 and 1980, and now account for half that country's oil consumption. Europe's dependence on Middle Eastern oil supplies is even greater than that of the United States. Western Europe now imports half the energy it uses. Only Norway and Britain are net exporters of energy.

Western Europe is more economical of energy than the United States. In West Germany, Britain or Sweden, a 1 per cent increase in gross national product 'costs' a 0.6 per cent or 0.7 per cent increase in energy consumption. In the USA, the ratio approaches unity. Indeed, between 1950 and 1970, the US gross national product rose by an average of 3.2 per cent a year, while energy use increased by 3.4 per cent a year.[1] Substantial efforts are now being made to improve the growth/energy ratio.

Oil prices will, to be sure, reflect changes in the world market. If the world recession lasts for several years demand for oil will decline, and both contract prices and free market prices will ease accordingly. What matters, however, is the general direction of oil prices. Given the rapid industrialization of some Third World countries and the dependence of modern farming methods on oil and oil-based fertilizers, it is highly unlikely that energy will again become cheap.

In *Thinking Through the Energy Problem*[2] Professor Thomas Schelling argues that there is no such thing as an energy gap, no difference between demand and supply that cannot be bridged by the price mechanism. Higher prices will make economic reserves of energy that are expensive to exploit or difficult of access, and they will then be exploited. Instances are oil shale, tar sands and unexploited coal reserves, all of them in abundant supply in North America, and, in the case of coal, in Britain too. There are, however, grave obstacles to the extensive production of oil from shale, or to a much greater dependence on coal. Oil shale and coal can be produced least expensively by surface stripping, a process that has a serious impact on the environment. The rehabilitation of surface-mined deposits is expensive and laborious. In short, the difference between the private cost of production and the social cost is very large indeed and, once the social cost is shouldered, exploitation becomes much less attractive. Furthermore, environmental lobbies – the 'green' movements – are much more powerful and influential than they used to be. They have shown themselves capable of delaying or even preventing new primary product or industrial development, as in the case of the pipeline from Alaska's North Shelf to the major industrial areas of the American West, or the search for an inland site for London's third airport. The en-vironmental lobbies would undoubtedly fight proposals for major oil shale and coal development, and would insist upon rehabili-tation if, despite their opposition, such proposals went ahead.

Coal is capable of being converted into a fuel similar to petrol – gasohol – which can be used in cars. But coal cannot provide a quick answer to current energy problems. A substantial expansion of coal production would run into two additional difficulties apart from those already described. The deep mining of coal is a hazardous and unattractive occupation. It is not easy to lure people into working underground, though ironically the recession is driving people into the pits where the chances of a secure job seem better. However, if there were alternative ways of earning a good living, many might choose not to stay. Coal also has environmental disadvantages other than the impact of strip mining and of deep mining on the locality. It is dirty to burn, though in the better-off Western countries the use of smokeless fuel and the filtering of smoke emissions are now required by law. (Industrial cities in China still look like Hudders-field or Halifax thirty years ago.) Moreover, its sulphur emissions are dangerous, and so, in the long run, is the carbon dioxide created by burning it; for carbon dioxide built up in the earth's atmosphere absorbs and then radiates heat, creating a greenhouse effect in which temperatures on the earth's surface will gradually rise. It is estimated that a fourfold increase in the annual amount of carbon fuel burned could increase mean surface temperatures by two or three degrees centigrade, and by as much as ten degrees centigrade at higher latitudes.[3] A big increase in the use of coal, especially if it were uncontrolled by environmental safeguards, would present the world with a whole range of new problems.

NUCLEAR POWER

Many governments have looked to nuclear power as the most acceptable form of energy to supplement conventional sources and eventually to replace them. The fuel source is fairly plentiful and in the case of the fast breeder reactor self-perpetuating, since fast breeders produce more plutonium than they consume. Nuclear power also appears clean to produce, though it has turned out to be much more expensive than was estimated when the first generating stations were built.

There is no need here to rehearse at length the problems associated with a major development of nuclear power. One is radioactivity, which is to be found in nuclear waste and which can persist for very long periods, hundreds or even thousands of years. No completely safe or satisfactory way has yet been found for dealing with radioactive waste. Waste with low levels of radioactivity is usually dumped in the sea or in official disposal sites. Public resistance to dumping is growing, to the point where several disposal sites in the USA were closed in 1980 by order of the state governors. Waste with high levels of radioactivity, which has aroused much more public alarm, is either retained on nuclear sites in 'ponds' or reprocessed, which still leaves residual waste. Investigations into the burying of vitrified material in the deep ocean or in non-porous rock have not yet come up with a convincing solution, though high-level waste is being pumped into geological formations in the USSR. Moreover, public resistance to the siting of disposal dumps or reprocessing plants is not only strengthening but is becoming more effectively organized. The

Land Government of Niedersachsen in West Germany shelved proposals for a nuclear fuel reprocessing centre at Gorleben in May 1979 in the face of well-organized resistance; while it was technically feasible, it was not at that time politically possible, according to the Land Prime Minister, Dr Ernst Albrecht. German radioactive waste is now being sent to France for reprocessing, though test boring for suitable waste sites continues.

In fact, high-level radioactive waste is probably not the most serious hazard associated with nuclear power generation. It is very small in quantity and therefore constitutes a containable problem. Low-level waste is much larger in quantity, and its disposal is becoming more and more controversial. At the Hanford Nuclear Center in Richland, Washington State, plutonium in waste that was not categorized as highly radioactive accumulated in an upper layer of the soil with which the waste was covered. According to the US Atomic Energy Commission, a chain reaction could have been triggered off. In Michigan and in northern New York toxic wastes from older industrial and chemical processes, some but not all radioactive, have been revealed as highly dangerous to the neighbourhoods in which they were casually dumped years ago.

Quite apart from the problems of disposing of radioactive waste materials, the operation of nuclear power stations carries enormous risks. Because of the destructive potential of nuclear power, the likelihood of an accident has to be reduced to negligible proportions. The Three Mile Island episode at Harrisburg in Pennsylvania in 1979 set back the US civil nuclear programme with its plans for eighty-eight additional nuclear power stations by many years. Few reports have appeared of a much more damaging accident near Kyshtym in the Soviet Union in the winter of 1957–8, though it is believed that thousands of square miles were rendered radioactive, and hundreds of people lost their lives.[4] Given the huge risks, nuclear power stations require high-precision engineering, highly skilled maintenance and minute dedication to the details of safety. Any technology needing such high standards over such a long period is bound to be worrying, if only because human beings are not totally reliable. The US Nuclear Regulatory Commission, commenting in November 1979 on Three Mile Island, remarked in the unattractive jargon of late-twentieth-century technology:

'Operations personnel must not have a mind-set that future accidents are impossible.' In July 1980, Britain's Nuclear Installations Inspectorate strongly criticized the management of the Windscale reprocessing plant; no one had noticed radioactive waste leaking into the ground over a period of many years.[5] The engineering problem worries those responsible for constructing and running nuclear power stations even more than the disposal of radioactive waste.

The unsolved, and perhaps insoluble, problems of nuclear power, which become more serious as the scale of operations mounts, suggest caution at the very least about pressing ahead with a major increase in nuclear power plants. Increasing dependence on this source of energy is a high-risk policy until much more is known.

CONSERVING RESOURCES

Renewable energy sources have been little used in recent decades, perhaps because windmills and watermills seem to belong to a pre-industrial past. Wind and water have the immense advantage of being inexhaustible, since they are in such abundant supply – at least in the West – that they are free or very inexpensive goods. But now the technologies of harnessing tidal power, wave power, and solar power are being vigorously developed. Israel and California both get over 10 per cent of their domestic heating from solar power. France has successfully generated electricity from the tides at La Rance in Brittany. Wave machines are being designed in Britain and in Scandinavia, where the turbulent North Sea, Baltic and Atlantic coasts offer potential sites for them. But none of these alternative sources can make a major impact on the supply of energy for a decade or more. While work on them obviously needs to be pushed ahead as a matter of urgency, the industrialized world for the next ten or twenty years will have to pay heavily for its energy. There may be no energy gap in the strict sense that the price mechanism will balance demand and supply; but the market's response to higher prices is likely to be delayed by the difficulties of increasing supply quickly and acceptably. As the US National Academy of Sciences' Energy Futures Panel put it, in its 1978 report, 'If we had decades, the market alone, working through gradual rises in prices, would be sufficient. But the decades are not there.'

Dearer energy has repercussions on food and raw material prices as well. Many minerals to be produced in a usable form demand colossal inputs of energy. Aluminium, for example, requires a great deal of electricity; copper has to be separated from the increasingly lean ore in which it is found, a process requiring a big energy input. Steel manufacture, especially by traditional processes, needs large quantities of coking coal and, of course, electricity as well. Energy costs are now also a large component of the cost of food production, both directly through the use of farm machinery and tractors and indirectly through fertilizers and animal feeding stuffs based on hydrocarbons. Compelled to maximize yields, Western farmers use huge quantities of fertilizers, pesticides and other chemicals on their fields. So increasingly do Soviet bloc farmers and those Third World farmers who have been caught up in the 'green revolution'. Higher oil prices therefore mean higher food prices in a large part of the world.

Energy resources – or more precisely, fossil fuels – are not the only resources under strain. The area of cultivable land, as Barbara Ward pointed out in her recent book, *Progress for a Small Planet*,[6] is shrinking owing to the inroads of urbanization and erosion. Cities in the Third World are exploding in size, haphazardly using up land once available for agriculture. The deserts and dustbowls are spreading, partly because of the rate at which trees and bushes are being cut down for fuel or for land clearance, partly because of soil exhaustion as a result of poor farming methods. Barbara Ward forecasts that the world's present area of cultivable land, estimated at 1,200 million hectares, will be halved by the end of the century.

Economic growth also impinges on mineral resources. In 1976, the United Nations Secretariat in its report on *The Future of the World Economy* estimated that the consumption of certain minerals, including copper, would be five times the 1970 volume in the year 2000. Energy use would double every sixteen years. Obviously the severe economic recession will reduce the demand well below that projected in 1976; yet a nasty dilemma remains. High growth will rapidly drive up input prices, making production costs more expensive. Low growth or decline may avoid that consequence but will not satisfy the expectations of the world's consumers. The Science Council of Canada, in a report entitled *Canada as a Conserver Society* (September 1977), observed: 'It is now understood that in many fields the continuing expansion of current practices will not be possible in the future.' The Council did not propose nil growth; rather it suggested that the key to prospering despite scarce resources is to be found in changing our current practices – in learning to use resources more frugally, in conserving those we have by re-using and recycling them, in designing buildings and artefacts and production processes to minimize resource demands. Prices, the Council recommended, should reflect total real costs, including the costs to society of, for example, pollution, and the costs to future generations of, for example, the running down of unrenewable fuel reserves.

I have argued that more expensive energy and other resources are likely to restrain economic growth, but they are by no means the only factors to do so. Rigidities in the market for goods and in the market for labour, described in Chapter 3, may distort the effect of a reduction in the money supply. They may also distort the effect of measures to stimulate growth, such as lower interest rates or higher public expenditure. Firms may raise prices rather than increase output. Trade unions may push up wages rather than create extra jobs. These rigidities, however, are not the main cause of the current economic recession. The main cause lies in the huge unused surpluses of the Middle Eastern oil producers, which sterilize a large part of the effective demand for the world's goods and services. Unless that demand is activated by lending to those who want to consume those goods and services, especially in the Third World, demand will fall below supply, and supply will be cut back. And that is exactly what is happening. The recession of 1979 deepened in 1980 and is likely to prove more severe and long-lasting than any of its post-war predecessors.

GROWTH SLOWS

The slowdown in economic growth is dramatic. The United States' gross national product fell by $\frac{3}{4}$ per cent in 1980, Britain's gross domestic product by $2\frac{1}{4}$ per cent. In 1981, a further decline of

2 per cent for Britain is forecast by the OECD.[7] The growth rate for the whole OECD area for 1980 was less than 1 per cent, compared to 4 per cent a year or more in the sixties and early 1970s. The economic projections for the years up to 1982 are little better; 1 per cent growth in 1981 and a slow recovery in 1982 is expected – but nothing resembling a return to the buoyant years before 1973.

The low or negative growth rate projected up to the end of 1982 poses a difficult challenge for socialists. These are years in which the burden of existing commitments to pensions and benefits, health and welfare services will become proportionately heavier in stagnating or declining economies. If socialists reject the dismantling of the welfare state, as they do, how can it be financed?

Even without growth, there is scope for increasing the yield of taxation to help maintain the level of public expenditure. Widening the tax base is a better place to begin than increasing the standard rate of income tax, given public resistance to high income taxes. The scope for widening the tax base differs. Some countries, such as Sweden and the Federal Republic of Germany, already have modest wealth taxes. Others, like Britain, do not. Some, like Britain and the United States, permit a whole range of allowances and expenditures to be set against tax, especially by companies or the self-employed. Widening the tax base to include a wealth tax on substantial fortunes, and simplifying the tax system by drastically narrowing allowances and permitted expenditure would be welcomed by a large number of taxpayers who resent the fact that they are not among those who can claim for cars, entertainment and accommodation, and who suspect that such concessions are widely abused.

Tax yields, however, in a slowly growing or a declining economy cannot be pushed up very far. So socialists will also have to be more critical of the way money is spent. The linking in Britain of civil service pensions to civil service pay, combined with the inflation-proofing of these pensions, is an example of an over-generous commitment. It will prove difficult to finance in the future. There also has to be some fundamental examination of the social services. Their purpose, the succour of the elderly, the ill, the disabled and the disadvantaged, is central to the socialist philosophy. But the social services do not always serve their clients as effectively as they serve their staffs. Socialists must be on guard against any transformation of social justice and community care into bureaucracy, which is expensive and self-perpetuating. This problem is explored in more detail in Chapter 10.

Slow growth does not only threaten public expenditure. It also closes the door on a solution to the looming issue of mass unemployment, at least if we use present policy tools. The OECD estimated in January 1979 that a rate of growth of $3\frac{1}{2}$ per cent in its member countries would be needed just to prevent the then existing levels of unemployment from worsening. Those 1978–9 levels were themselves historically high, ranging from $3\frac{1}{2}$ per cent in the Federal Republic of Germany to 7 per cent in the United States and Britain, and 8 per cent in Denmark. In 1978, the Western world had entered a difficult period in which the number of young people coming into the labour force began to expand rapidly – the children of the baby boom of the late 1950s and early 1960s. This period of 'young adult' population growth lasts up to 1984. Furthermore, the substantial increase in those seeking work coincides with a drop in those reaching retirement age, for today's elderly workers were born in the years of the First World War and its immediate aftermath, when birth rates were low. The rise in the number of young people looking for work, the drop in the numbers reaching retirement age, and the depressingly low growth projections combine to create, at least potentially, a gravely serious unemployment problem.

WORKING WOMEN

Added to these factors is another relatively new phenomenon affecting employment, certainly very different from anything experienced in the 1930s. This is the social revolution among women, in particular married women, most of whom are no longer willing to stay at home. It is a phenomenon much more marked in Britain, the USA and the Scandinavian countries than in West Germany or Italy. The number of working women in Britain has risen by nearly three millions in the post-war years, and in the United States by some thirteen millions.

Table 1, quite apart from illustrating a social revolution, also

Table 1. Participation of Women in Paid Employment 1950–77

	1950	1977	Difference 1950–77	Percentage growth 1950–77
Germany	44.3	48.4	+ 4.1	9.25
France	49.5	50.1	+ 0.6	1.2
UK	40.7	57.3	+ 16.6	40.1
Sweden	35.1	70.0	+ 34.9	98.9
USA	37.2	55.7	+ 18.5	49.7
Italy	32.0	37.1	+ 5.1	15.9

Number of people seeking or holding jobs represented by a 1 per cent increase equals (approximately)

Germany	200,000
France	165,000
UK	170,000
Sweden	25,000
USA	720,000
Italy	190,000

Source: Organization for Economic Cooperation and Development.

tells us something about the comparative record of unemployment of the different countries in the West. I do not believe that any policy short of compulsion can make women who have decided to take a job go back to the kitchen sink; but we should recognize, in describing these comparative unemployment levels, that some countries have taken on board the revolution of sexual equality and the desire or need of many women to work for wages, while others have yet to do so.

Full employment will be difficult to restore, given more young people, large and still rising numbers of married women wanting jobs, and low or nil growth. It has become fashionable to declare that full employment is unattainable, that the existing work must be shared out, or even that we should educate young people to accept long periods of unemployment or enforced leisure. Yet the work ethic is strong. People are judged by what they do and, more important, they judge themselves by the same criterion. The self-confidence of men and women is related to their contribution to the community. There is no way out of this by providing them with such levels of unemployment benefit or welfare that they will have a sufficient income to remain at leisure all their days. Maybe we can change the pattern of work; maybe we can shorten the working week or, more likely, the working life. Maybe our values will change. But democratic governments cannot escape the responsibility of trying to find work for those who want it.

INITIATIVES

The next two years are likely to be harsh and disagreeable. Reductions in investment programmes and in social expenditure will reinforce the recession by further reducing demand. Unemployment will go higher, especially among vulnerable groups like young people and those without educational qualifications. Worried about payments deficits, countries will try to discourage demand at home, while engaging in yet fiercer battles for highly competitive export markets. In the short run, the only initiative that could radically alter the world's economic prospects would be the recycling of the oil exporters' surpluses as well as some of the currency reserves of the industrial countries to create a vast new market in the developing countries, in effect the Brandt Commission's proposals in their most radical form. Simply to state such proposals is to emphasize how improbable their adoption is, despite growing public understanding and support.

Short of such a radical policy, sound economic management would encourage more economical use of energy and raw materials and would emphasize conservation and recycling. It would adopt those new technologies or new versions of old technologies which make fewest demands on scarce resources. It would enable a steady growth rate to be restored once the recession has come to an end. As the Science Council of Canada pointed out, a sensible awareness that fossil fuels and mineral supplies are limited, and that the environment has a finite capacity to restore itself, could lead to a self-sustaining world economy in which there could be steady if modest growth. Given, too, a greater willingness to train and retrain people and to develop skill-intensive processes and products.

something close to full employment, or at least the right to employment for those who wanted it, could be restored. But there are many lessons to be learned first. The industrial countries have been wildly profligate in the booming post-war decades. Their governments and their peoples have enjoyed a material spree never paralleled before. Now, as the late Anthony Crosland said to Britain's local authorities in 1977, the party is over. In the United States and Britain, the public reaction to this news has been a mixture of remorse and refusal to listen. Conservative governments are now offering the strong medicine of unemployment and bankruptcy, as if governments' role was that of a Victorian nanny. The real need, however, is for a sober understanding of how the world has changed and an economic policy of modest self-sustaining growth that can accommodate to it.

5

The New Technologies

Until the breakthrough of the early 1970s into microelectronics, most new technologies were capital intensive – that is to say, they involved the substitution of plant and machinery for labour. They were also expensive. More sophisticated machinery replaced less advanced machinery, producing more but also costing more. Machine tools, at first mechanical, then electro-mechanical, are a good example. The cost of starting a new firm or retooling an old plant became higher and higher, penalizing the small entrepreneur who had no access to large capital sums.

Microelectronic devices, however, are highly adaptable and remarkably cheap. Unlike earlier advances in technology, they do not simply substitute capital for labour; they save capital, labour, space and often raw materials too. Their major input is knowledge and information. Hence the phrase, the information society, to describe the microelectronic future. So dramatic has been the drop in cost that microelectronic devices will be able to be very widely used in a great range of applications. A single function on a microchip costs less than a thousandth as much as did a single transistor function twenty years ago. The microchip is tiny compared to the transistor, itself small in relation to the valve, and the raw materials involved in its manufacture, mainly silicon, are cheap and abundant.

Microelectronics are also revolutionary in their implications for society. In manufacturing, microprocessor controls are likely to improve the performance of a wide range of products, from domestic appliances to heavy construction machinery and motorcars. They will also radically alter manufacturing processes. Assembly lines can be automated by the use of robots fitted with microelectronic sensors that enable them to be used in a range of tasks. Computer-controlled machine tools are much more adaptable than numerically controlled machine tools. Microelectronics can also cut the cost of the expensive elements in automatic processes, control and inspection. Computer-aided design eliminates much of the detailed draughtsmanship and technical drawing required for traditional design, and makes a direct link between the designer and the production manager. It brings individually designed products within the range of a much larger market.

Microprocessors will have a major impact on office work, making such familiar skills as filing or shorthand typing obsolete within a few years. Data recorded on magnetic tape is available almost instantaneously. Administrators and executives will be able to get up-to-date displays of accounts and sales records on their desk terminals. Managers will summon computer printouts showing in exact detail what stage a manufacturing process has reached, or how many of any given item have been produced. They will convey their own decisions by programming their own computer in simple language. As machines become capable of recognizing individual voices and responding to them, people will be able to dictate directly to automatic typewriters, or to instruct computers over a telephone. Such techniques are beginning to be used in banking, giving immediate access to customers' accounts, in insurance and in commercial services. The microelectronic office will be as different from the traditional office of filing cabinets and typing pools as the car is from the horse-drawn carriage.

Microelectronics open the gateway to the whole kingdom of information and also guides the searcher to what he or she wants. Viewdata systems – such as British Telecom's Prestel – are already on the market, their coverage limited only because the information provided by those who supply it is limited. Subscribers can select the type of information they want, for instance stock-exchange prices or the latest news. They can use the system to tell them whether places are available at a chosen theatre or on an aeroplane, and then book directly through the system, quoting a credit card number. The technology is capable of handling very large quantities of data indeed, and of frequently updating it. Viewdata systems can be linked through to computerized storage systems, enabling researchers to get detailed information about any of the subjects covered. Through the microfiles of library systems with an international coverage, like that of the US Library of Congress or the British Library's Blaise system, people will be able to obtain details of all publications in their field of interest, including scientific papers and newspaper articles.

SOCIAL EFFECTS

The social effects of the new technologies are likely to be immense. Based as they are on rapid and easily accessible communications, the new technologies will free industry and the services from the constraints of location. Most work nowadays is centralized in factories or offices, to take advantage of expensive plant and machinery or to facilitate communication between people. Men and women travel to their work. Work done at home is often a throwback to an earlier industrial age, when knitters and glove-makers did their own spinning and tanning. Home-workers are usually ill-organized and badly paid. Yet the new technologies may revive working from home. Inexpensive computer terminals can be installed in a home or a range of small separate offices. Linked to one another by telephone lines based on optic fibres, each cable carrying thousands of separate lines, scores of people will be able to confer with one another without being physically in the same place. Thus microprocessors could bring about the gradual destruction of the city, if people prefer to live in villages or small towns. The erosion of jobs in the old inner cities may become even more acute, requiring new and radical approaches to the question of how the cities are to be sustained and redeveloped. On the other hand, the decentralization of work and decision-making ceases to be a dream. Human beings can be made whole again, working and living in the same community. Microelectronics offer the opportunity of reuniting the family, and making commuting an obsolete and unnecessary activity.

The achievement of full employment will not at first be made easier by the advent of the new technologies. They will create jobs, most of them in the information sector – for example in systems analysis, software design and data processing – but they will destroy others, especially routine office work like shorthand, typing and filing, and repetitive manufacturing jobs like assembling components. Some skilled jobs are threatened too, for instance technical drawing and stock control.

So far microelectronics have not had a significant effect on employment in Britain, though they are beginning to alter employment patterns in some other countries. The Central Policy Review Staff (CPRS) undertook a study of the consequences of microelectronics on Britain in 1978.[1] In its study, the Central Policy Review Staff pointed out that microelectronics are primarily being used for improving the quality, reliability and efficiency of existing products and processes. The study gave as instances better stock control, allowing businesses to operate with less stock; the extension of services, for instance in banking and insurance; and in booking and accounting systems for small hotels and the entertainment industry.

As microprocessors are more widely introduced, however, jobs in some occupations are bound to become redundant. At a time of high unemployment, there will be powerful pressures to resist the introduction of these technologies. But advanced industrial countries cannot risk rejecting microelectronics. Any industrialized country that fails to improve its processes and products by the use of microprocessors will lose markets and jobs to its competitors. Given the speed at which some Third World countries are industrializing, the older industrial countries will not find it easy to retain their foothold in traditional manufacturing and will have to move on to more sophisticated areas. Bluntly, there is no rational alternative to adopting the new technologies. The debate should be about what social and industrial policies will most effectively ease the transition. Andrew Likierman, a lecturer at the London Business School, put it this way: 'In the economy as a whole, the factor above all which will determine the net employment effect will be how fast industry adapts in relation to its overseas competitors.'[2] It may nevertheless be true that on balance jobs will be lost even by countries that do adapt, simply because the new technologies require less labour. There is evidence that there will be a substantial loss of jobs in the industries most affected. The evidence in Britain comes from the manufacturers of telecommunications equipment. The switch from electro-mechanical equipment to electronic equipment for tele-phone exchanges greatly reduced the need for labour in the manufacturing plants. In 1978, hundreds of workers were declared redundant by Standard Telephone and Cables for this very reason. Once installed, the new equipment also needs fewer people to operate it and is easier to maintain.

Evidence from West Germany, which is more advanced in microelectronics than Britain, tells a similar story. In the years between 1970 and 1977, output of office machines and data processors, an industry into which microelectronics has penetrated, increased 49 per cent; the volume of employment (numbers of employees multiplied by hours worked) fell by 27.5 per cent. By comparison, in German mining and manufacturing generally, production rose by 13.5 per cent in those years, while employment fell 14.5 per cent and the volume of employment by 21.3 per cent.[3]

NEW JOBS

The additional demand for people to take up jobs related to the new technologies is not likely to offset all the job losses. Until recently, the rise in service employment – in the public service, hotels and catering, banking and insurance and the professions – has more than offset the decline in employment in manufacturing and the primary sectors of mining and agriculture. In Britain, jobs in the service sector increased by an average of 152,000 a year between 1972 and 1978, while jobs in manufacturing fell by 136,000 a year. Four fifths of the twelve million new jobs created in the USA between 1970 and 1979 were in the service sector. But microelec-tronics and telecommunications may have their greatest impact here. The greatest impact predicted in West Germany, for instance, is on administration. The German company Siemens AG estimates that 43 per cent of office jobs can be standardized and 25–30 per cent automated by the end of the 1980s. The figures are much higher for public administration. This implies that the introduction of automatic typewriters replacing electric manually-operated typewriters, microfilms and printouts replacing files and xeroxes, and direct person-to-person transmissions using visual displays instead of letters and telexes could cut office employment at every level by a third or more.

The calculations by Siemens AG are corroborated by a more extensive survey covering the European Community, the United States, Canada, Japan, Sweden and Norway. The survey, which was done in 1980 by a major international management consultancy organization, Metra International, showed that in some sectors over half the jobs both in offices and in industry could disappear in the next five to ten years. Banking and insurance, process industries, retailing and transport are likely to be among the sectors particularly affected. Jobs for production workers and for machine-tool operators will suffer as computer-controlled machines are introduced; these can save as much as 80 per cent of the labour needed in traditional processes. Automated assembly lines using robots need only one human employee for every five needed now.

Nevertheless, there will be a need for thousands more workers in microelectronics-related fields. Vacancies for computer programmers, systems analysts, electronic technicians and design engineers are hard to fill; the supply is much less than the demand. The new technologies put a premium on skilled and qualified people. They offer few opportunities for the unskilled and the uneducated.

The old industrialized countries, like Britain, have a workforce much of which is unskilled, and some of which is skilled in traditional trades that are becoming obsolete. The mismatch between those seeking jobs and the jobs on offer becomes more acute year by year. Countries with extensive training systems, like West Germany and Switzerland, can emphasize study of new technologies in their vocational education courses and alter the balance of apprenticeships offered as between different occupations. The information society requires better educated young people with a broad and flexible vocational foundation. Yet even West Germany is hampered by the narrowness and specificity of some of its apprenticeship training. Because changes are coming so fast, industrial economies can only remain competitive by continuous updating of skills and knowledge, which has come to be known as continuing education. Sweden has a highly developed system for retraining adult workers, in which 2 per cent of the workforce are in training at any one time. This should make the transition to a new employment pattern relatively painless.

Countries able to take advantage of microelectronics and other related technologies because they are well provided with training and retraining systems and have good relations between management and workpeople may be able to create enough new jobs to offset those that are lost. Microelectronics encourage decentralization. They can be used economically in small-scale batch production or even to make individual products like garments or machines. The prospects for new small enterprises are therefore bright, and such small enterprises are significant creators of new jobs. Taken all in all, microelectronics may eventually be neutral or even positive in their consequences for employment.

But that cannot be said of countries or industries with inadequate means of training for new skills, or where profound suspicions lead to unwillingness to use new technologies efficiently. In such countries and industries a mismatch between the skills that do exist and the skills that the new technologies require will multiply the consequences for unemployment. Some people will offer skills no one any longer needs. Investors will look elsewhere because of the lack of the relevant skills to operate the new technologies and potential jobs will be lost in consequence. The new technologies could widen the discrepancies between the industrial countries further unless immediate steps are taken to raise the standard and quality of skill training in those that lag behind.

Microelectronics have attracted a great deal of notice, yet they are only one of a large family of new technologies. Robots, mentioned above, are being used in the car industry for repetitive and unattractive jobs like paint-spraying and assembly. Clearly robots can replace people; but, so far at least, they have mainly been used in processes for which it was hard to recruit or where turnover was high. If the new technologies threaten some traditional jobs in factories and offices, they also promise to moderate the industrial world's dependence on fossil fuels and other non-renewable raw materials. Electronic devices will enable vehicles to use petroleum more economically by regulating engine speed; computers can provide constantly updated information about the least congested routes between two points, saving fuel on many journeys. Better calibrated stock control reduces waste of food and raw materials. Likewise developments in materials and materials handling promise significant savings. Raw materials are being used in much more economical ways. Shaped solid objects are increasingly made by moulding and extruding (polymers) or by precision casting (metals), rather than by milling, turning or cutting. Foamed and ribbed forms use less raw materials than solid forms. Expensive minerals, like coal, can be mixed with inexpensive materials, like sand, to economize on prime fuel consumption, as is done with fluid-bed combustion, a method of producing heat and power that can also use a wide variety of fuels, including domestic rubbish. Recycling of waste is another rapidly advancing technology. Not only can the residue be used for district heating once recoverable materials have been extracted; a lot of biological waste can be used as a source of food for animals.

BIOTECHNOLOGY

A more radical alternative source of fuel and food may emerge from the new discipline of biotechnology, producing protein from hydrocarbons and fuel from plant waste or from algae. Biotechnology uses the techniques of genetic manipulation to develop new products from biological materials, such as bacteria and plant and animal cells. The potential is immense. Algae, the green scum on stagnant ponds, can be grown artificially in any space open to sunlight. All that is needed in addition to sunlight is carbon dioxide and some kind of nutrient solution. Such is their versatility that they can be converted into methane, a fuel source, into starch or animal feed. Fuel cells using methanol, a derivative of methane, could be a pollution-free source of energy, both cheaper and more efficient than the conventional systems now in use. Enzymes are highly versatile, and can be used to recycle waste and in fermentation processes.

A report published in April 1980 by a joint working party of ACARD (Advisory Council for Applied Research and Development), the Royal Society and the ABRC (Advisory Board for the Research Councils) said, 'We envisage biotechnology as creating wholly novel industries, with low fossil energy demands, which will be of key importance to the world economy in the next century.'[4] Organic chemicals, according to the report, can be made much more economically by biological processes than by current production from oil feedstocks. Indeed, the implications of biotechnology are as far-reaching as are those of microelectronics, though their realization is more distant in time. Biotechnology holds out the prospect of a world emancipated from want, with virtually limitless supplies of fuel and food. As the world lurches into a painful awareness of the scarcity of resources, the restless pursuers of knowledge have once again come up with solutions, but solutions that can only be useful if political and industrial leaders understand and encourage them.

The new technologies, like all technologies, are morally neutral. Whether their advent makes the world a better place or not depends on the uses to which they are put. And that, in turn, depends upon the decisions of many people, especially of politicians, managers, trade union leaders, engineers and scientists. In Chapter 1, I argued that earlier technologies shaped society – that human beings had been subordinated to technology. The new technologies, cheap, flexible, dependent on knowledge and information as their main input, can free human beings from many of their current constraints, for instance constraints of resources, geography and location. But the new technologies could also enable those with power to control their fellow-citizens more effectively than in even the most efficient dictatorships of the past. They could impoverish large sections of the community by destroying jobs. The information society will make colossal demands on our imagination and ingenuity and on the capacity of our institutions to respond to new challenges. The most immediate of those challenges is what to do about unemployment.

6

The Threat of Unemployment

For a generation after the war, full employment was one important measure of a good and socially just society. The work of Keynes and Beveridge suggested that full employment would be attainable in a largely market economy, provided the government was willing to intervene, if necessary, to create adequate demand.

It is now quite widely believed that full employment can no longer be achieved, at least not without a drastic redefinition of what constitutes full-time work. The late Hannah Arendt asked what would happen when 'the work society runs out of work'. Clive Jenkins and Barry Sherman wrote a book on the impact of microelectronics on employment, starkly entitled *The Collapse of Work*.[1] It may even be that more and more people do not want to work. Exponents of this view range from those on the political right who believe that Western economies carry a great burden of layabouts and scroungers, to those of more radical tendencies who welcome the collapse of the work ethic and the coming of a world of constructive and creative leisure. Such facts as are available support neither view. In spite of energetic efforts to locate them, few scroungers and layabouts are ever found and prosecuted; as a proportion of all those unemployed, their numbers are low indeed. Nor is there much evidence that, once offered a reasonable job, people prefer leisure. Work instills self-respect; it is a means of defining who one is and what one can attain. A world without work would be one in which most people would be profoundly unhappy, bored and purposeless.

It is of course true that a growing number of people dislike the formal labour market system, with its hierarchies of management, foremen and shopfloor workers. Young people in particular are attracted to other styles of work, for instance in cooperatives, communes or small self-employed groups engaged in everything from making rock music to cleaning offices. But the rejection of formal industrial structures is not the same as the rejection of work. It is rather a challenge to those who are responsible for managing industry and the unions to find more acceptable and humane ways of working.

SHORT-TERM MEASURES

Most Western governments since the war have regarded full employment as an important policy objective. Meanwhile, they have found ways of softening the sharp economic edges of unemployment by relating unemployment benefit to earnings, by easing entitlement to unemployment benefit and by introducing the right to redundancy pay: in effect, buying off those about to lose their jobs. In return, throughout the 1970s, unemployed men and women were politically quiescent. Unemployment was, until the late 1970s, rarely a major issue at elections.

Most government measures in the 1970s were directed at transitional unemployment, because most unemployment was temporary, a gap between jobs. But now the number of long-term unemployed is rising, although in Britain the proportion remains between a fifth and a quarter of all unemployed people. In October 1980, 378,000 people in Britain had been jobless for over a year.[2] Those who have been unemployed for over a year are in a grim position. They are no longer entitled to earnings-related benefit, and their redundancy money and tax credits will probably have been spent. The decline in the number of vacancies means that there is little hope of finding another job. Those who lose their jobs now may be unemployed for a long time. Whether they will remain quiescent in these circumstances is doubtful. Governments, however, have only recently encountered high and lasting unemployment; they have not yet altered their policies to take account of this new and disturbing phenomenon.

Throughout the 1960s, unemployment in Western Europe rarely

exceeded 5 per cent, and in most countries most of the time remained below 3 per cent. After 1975 unemployment, fuelled by the recession, increased rapidly. By the end of the 1970s, the United States, the United Kingdom and France were all experiencing unemployment rates of 6 per cent or more, with much higher rates among young people and in the economically depressed regions. A whole armoury of new measures was used by governments to try to keep unemployment down: regional investment incentives, public works programmes and factories built in advance of requirements, to mention only three. For the most volatile group, young men and women in the first few years after leaving school, special measures have been adopted. West Germany expanded her apprenticeship system, the United States experimented with ways of keeping young people in school by guaranteeing them part-time jobs outside school hours and Britain offered every young person still out of work a guarantee of a training place or a work experience place no later than the Easter after the date at which he or she left school. The informal economy, which is outside the legal corset of the tax and insurance systems, also absorbed a lot of unemployed people, especially the young and the old, though these unofficial jobs, just because they are unofficial, do not show up in the statistics.

Despite all these measures, however, the outlook is bleak. The first half of the 1980s offers a discouraging prospect of low or nil growth, and a still-increasing working population. In the United States, Canada and Britain, the gross national product is constant or negative in 1980 and 1981, though the effect on unemployment will be mitigated by low productivity. West Germany has the obverse problem – a continued rise in productivity that can only be translated into more jobs if markets for German products expand very quickly too.

Forecasts of unemployment show an upward spiral, with figures for Britain exceeding 11 per cent by the end of 1981. Estimates published in December 1980 show twenty-three million unemployed in OECD countries, which could increase to twenty-five and a half millions by the middle of 1982.[3] Most disturbing of all are the estimates for youth unemployment, expected by the OECD in 1981 to exceed 16 per cent in France and Britain, and 15 per cent in the United States. Such levels recall the Great

Depression. Nor are they the highest. In Italy and Spain, one young person in five is already out of work; among American young black men, one in three.[4]

The gloomy growth picture coincides with a growing population of working age. The young people born during the baby boom of the late 1950s and early 1960s (the high birth rate came to an end in 1962 and was followed in the late 1960s and early 1970s by a dramatic decline) have been entering the labour market in the last three years, and will continue to do so until 1983–4. Their entry coincides with a decline in retirement numbers, reflecting the low birth rates of the 1914–18 period. In Britain, the Department of Employment estimates that there will be 1.1 million more men and women in the labour force in 1982 than there were in 1976. Half of them – 565,000 – will be under twenty-four. To this demographically based expansion of the labour force must be added the consequences of the still rapidly rising entry of married women into the labour force. Between July 1978 and July 1979, 2.7 million new jobs were created in the USA but the number of unemployed declined by only 300,000. Married women entering the labour market accounted for much of the difference.

By the middle of the 1980s, the worst of unemployment among young people should be over. Much reduced age groups will then enter the labour market, and the upsurge of employment activity among married women is likely to have levelled out. Some labour market economists even predict that there may be a shortage of young workers. The danger is that the baby-boom generation, many unskilled and with a history of unemployment or only intermittent employment, may become a permanent problem, hard to employ and hard to absorb into society. For them, a second chance of education or training is going to be very important.

Britain's poor prospects for employment in the 1980s are compounded by two other developments. High interest rates, the outcome of tight monetary policies directed against inflation, discourage capital investment. Although Britain has the oldest capital equipment of all the industrialized countries, investment is likely to decline for several years. Investment, both residential and non-residential, is sluggish in most major OECD countries owing to the weakness of market demand.

The other development is also a consequence of policies to curb inflation. Public expenditure has been reined back in Britain as in most Western countries, sometimes as a direct outcome of government policies, sometimes because of financial prudence, sometimes because of action by legislators reflecting grassroots feeling among taxpayers or even contemporary intellectual fashion. In the United States, for instance, many state legislatures have imposed limits on spending or enjoined balanced budgets. In short, as private consumption declines, neither investment nor public expenditure is likely to compensate for that decline.

YOUTH UNEMPLOYMENT

Unemployment by no means affects all workers equally. It is misleading to think of the workforce as homogeneous; it is more and more segmented. Young people between sixteen and twenty-four suffer disproportionately when the economy slows down; youth unemployment typically is two or three times higher than adult unemployment.* The exceptions are the Federal Republic of Germany, Austria and Switzerland, all countries that have adapted the medieval system of apprenticeship to modern conditions. Among young people the least educated and especially the least educated girls are the hardest hit; as for ethnic minority youngsters without skills, it is almost impossible for them to get decent jobs. Unqualified young people tend to move from one dead-end or unsatisfactory job to another, rarely spending more than six months in any one job, drifting in and out of work and in and out of the labour market. This rather aimless in-and-out pattern is much more usual than long unbroken periods of unemployment, the fate of a relatively small minority.

Some young people may not be damaged by the experience of repeated short periods out of work; moving from job to job and from place to place may even allow them to try out different kinds of work until they find out what appeals to them most. But these periods in between jobs are getting longer and longer. The number of young people under twenty-four who had been without a job for a year or

* In Britain, unemployment among under-eighteens was 12 per cent and among eighteen to twenties 10 per cent, in August 1979; the national unemployment rate was 5.5 per cent.[5]

more rose more than ten times over in Britain during the 1970s, and is still increasing. Like the growing minority of long-term unemployed, many young people lose confidence and finally abandon themselves to apathy, making a living out of odd jobs, whatever their families can spare and intermittent unemployment insurance or welfare payments. Being out of work confirms the low opinion such youngsters have of their own abilities, and seems to them to justify the modesty of their aspirations. Creating self-confidence has to be a main objective of any policy for young people, and it should start in the schools.

Better educated boys and girls do stand a reasonable chance of a job in most OECD countries, but graduates may have to lower their sights. As in the United States and Canada, graduates in Western Europe are now competing for jobs as technicians, technologists, foremen, health ancillary workers and skilled workers with those holding vocational qualifications. In West Germany, some boys and girls qualified to enter university have gone into an apprenticeship first. In Italy and Spain, many graduates can find no work at all. These young people, usually the sons and daughters of professional middle-class parents, are raw material for social unrest, more so than the unqualified unemployed, for their expectations are much higher and their anger at being unwanted consequently greater.

Before turning to what governments have done and can do about unemployment, one more comment on the labour market may be illuminating. In the last twenty years, the position of people who already possess a job has been strengthened in all sorts of ways. Laws have been passed to underpin job security, for instance by making it difficult to dismiss employees once taken on, and by requiring long notice of redundancy or a consultative procedure before redundancies are declared. In addition, the financial penalties for dismissing an employee are now considerable, at any rate in the industrialized European countries where provision exists for redundancy pay and transfer of pension rights. Collective bargaining often ensures additional severance pay, silver or bronze hand-shakes. In some industries, dismissed employees are entitled to have their incomes made up to 85 or 90 per cent of their earnings when in work. Such laws and practices are well-intentioned. But by putting a premium on job-holding, and by making the decision to employ an extra person much more like a capital investment, they discourage the recruitment of new entrants to the labour force. Indeed, employers themselves may actively encourage turnaround among their young workers to avoid acquiring a whole range of legal obligations towards them.

Young people's employment is discouraged too by heavy non-wage costs, such as national insurance or social security contributions paid by the employer, training costs, holiday pay and pensions. In the 1950s, young people's wages were lower in relation to adult wages than they are today, and non-wage costs were very much less. Young people are more expensive on both counts than they were; if they are also believed to be less reliable, less productive and more trouble than older workers, including married women, the difference in cost no longer tips the balance in their favour.

Governments since 1973 have been torn between policies to stimulate growth and employment, and policies to curb inflation. As I pointed out in Chapter 2, there is no longer a simple choice to be made, since inflation can co-exist with high unemployment, partly because of the institutional rigidities in advanced economies I have described. Characteristically, governments have leaned towards anti-inflationary measures until unemployment rose so high that it became a political threat. Then they have relaxed monetary control, run budget deficits and even encouraged public investment and public works. The conservative mood of the late 1970s has strengthened governments' resistance to reflationary policies. Yet by the winter of 1980 only the British government was still cleaving to the strict monetarist line, despite heading into catastrophic rates of unemployment in some regions. And even the British government was modifying its stance at the microeconomic level.

THE YOUTH OPPORTUNITIES PROGRAMME

The British Labour governments of 1974–9 tried out a wide range of employment schemes, which stopped unemployment going up and even reduced it for young people. The most radical of these schemes was the Youth Opportunities Programme. The Youth

Opportunities Programme is one of the special schemes developed by the Manpower Services Commission (MSC), the agency responsible for the public employment and training services in Britain. There are ten commissioners appointed by the Secretary of State for Employment. One is the chairman; three are appointed after consultation with the Trades Union Congress, three after consultation with the Confederation of British Industry, two after consultation with the local authority associations, and one represents educational interests. Starting as a means of combining several disparate schemes of short industrial training, industrial workshops and work experience, the Youth Opportunities Programme broadened into a combination of a guarantee to young unemployed people and a structural transition from school to work. The original scheme was to provide 187,000 places for young people in 1978/9, at a cost of £113m, rising to 230,000 places the following year. Under pressure from the Department of Employment and the government, the concept of an Easter guarantee was introduced – that no boy or girl leaving school in July and still unemployed the following Easter would be without the offer of a short industrial training course or a work experience place by that time.

The scheme was remarkably successful. In its first year of operation, 162,000 young people entered the scheme, two thirds of them in work experience places on employers' premises. The Easter guarantee was almost wholly honoured. Equally impressive were the results of a follow-up survey of young people, previously unemployed, who had been through work experience schemes in September and October 1978. These showed 72 per cent had gone into jobs after completing work experience; another 12 per cent were either employed or in full-time further education or on another MSC course at the time the survey was done. The scheme's second year was even more successful, only 485 young people being without the offer of a place by March 1980. The Manpower Services Commission added a new guarantee to the long-term young unemployed, promising a place on the programme to any young person out of work for twelve months or more. This second guarantee slashed the number of long-term unemployed young people (under the age of nineteen) from 9,000 in July 1979 to 2,600 in April 1980.[6]

The Easter guarantee, brought forward to Christmas from 1981 on, is an attractive and exciting feature of the Youth Opportunities Programme, but it is not its major contribution to the problems of youth unemployment. For the Youth Opportunities Programme is essentially a short-term, remedial scheme, incapable of dealing with prolonged high levels of unemployment. Its lasting value lies in the creation, almost as a by-product, of an effective transitional step from school to work. A third of the young people on work experience schemes in 1978/9 got jobs with their sponsors. That demonstrated the importance of a period of familiarization: for the young person, discovering what behaviour is expected in holding down a job; for the employer, the contribution the young person can make before a final commitment is made to a permanent job. Nothing has shown so clearly the inadequacy of the abrupt transition in Britain from school to work; and it is precisely the less academic and less qualified young people for whom that transition in the past has been so sudden.

The Youth Opportunities Programme has taught the country other lessons. The concept of the guarantee compelled the Commission to make provision for all unemployed young people including the least qualified ones, the 'rough and tumble'. Many of these youngsters had no educational qualifications at all; some could barely read or write, let alone understand basic mathematics. It emerged that little was known about how to train or prepare for work youngsters in the lowest sector of academic ability. Providing courses of remedial education and off-the-job training able to meet the needs of the young unemployed is a need that is only now beginning to be met. Indeed, the British educational system, with its overwhelming emphasis on academic achievement rather than practical or vocational competence, has in the past shown little interest in doing so.

The work experience scheme, which absorbs the majority of young unemployed people in the Youth Opportunities Programme, offers lessons too. The cooperation extended by the TUC and the CBI at central level has not been universally followed by individual firms and trade unions. Indeed work experience schemes have been largely offered by small companies. 'Instead of the dozens or hundreds of youngsters that MSC expected to place with large firms, we are in fact placing boys and girls in ones and twos with little firms,' said Richard O'Brien, the chairman of MSC in 1979. There are two reasons for this, both with a much wider significance. One is the managerial structure of large firms; it is hard to find out who decides to take on work experience youngsters, and even when a decision is made, it is hard to get it carried out. Briefly, the decision-making systems and communication lines of large companies are so extended and slow that getting effective work experience schemes requires disproportionate time and effort. Second, large firms are nervous about union reactions; even a hint of opposition or objection from stewards or union representatives will cause them to withdraw offers of places. Nationalized industries are like other large firms in these respects, and their contribution to work experience schemes has been thin. Nor has the public service sector been helpful; in particular the biggest civil service union, CPSA, at first opposed work experience schemes for clerical work and refused to cooperate on them; hence there were no such work experience schemes in the civil service until 1980.

The Youth Opportunities Programme has justified itself in spite of these obstacles, and should be a permanent element in employment policy. It is, however, like all the other schemes mentioned above, essentially an expedient for dealing with transitional or short-term unemployment. Such schemes can take thousands, even hundreds of thousands, off the unemployment register for a while. They can, more ambitiously, make real inroads into structural unemployment, by providing remedial education and 'socialization' courses for disadvantaged or unqualified young people. But they cannot increase the number of permanent job opportunities in society.

TRAINING FOR SKILLS

One common phenomenon in Britain and other industrial countries is that even during periods of recession, certain skills remain in short supply. Indeed, the shortages may be so serious that new investment in job-creating industry or services is inhibited. Employers may cease to train during a recession; several years later, when the recovery comes, there is not enough skilled manpower. The fear of unemployment can also become the cause of unemployment. Workpeople will resist shortened periods of apprenticeship or adult retraining courses on the grounds that those coming out of them are not fully time-served craftsmen. Yet semiskilled job opportunities are lost for lack of a core of skilled men and women. True, considerable efforts have been made to expand industrial training. There was the establishment of Industrial Training Boards, the levy and grant system – which was much resented but right – the expansion of Skill Centres, the TOPs schemes for adults; and to some extent industry responded. But there has also been a great deal of resistance to change.

Some skilled workers have refused to work with adults trained in Skill Centres, because they have not 'served their time', the four or five years of the traditional apprenticeship. Skilled men and women trained in a much shorter time, it is argued, will dilute the status of the craftsman and undermine his position. The resistance is strongest where apprenticeships are the traditional destination of the able youngster, as in the north-east, and where unemployment is high. Yet even in these areas there have been severe shortages of skilled people and these shortages have discouraged investment in new plants and new jobs.

Employers for their part have failed to recognize the crucial role that training plays in economic competitivity. A few firms do more than their fair share of training, and often it is training of a very high quality. Others simply poach the skilled people they need by offering higher wages while undertaking no training themselves. Some industries, such as construction, traditionally had a core of craftsmen and then relied upon casual unskilled labour for the rest of the work. They saw no point in training them. Industries disliked the levy–grant system, introduced in 1966, which levied all the firms in an industry and paid grants to those who undertook training. The scheme was very much weakened in 1973, and a ceiling of 1 per cent of turnover was put on the levy. Firms undertaking their own training could be exempted from the levy altogether.

Most school-leavers in Britain, apart from those (14 per cent in 1980) lucky enough to get apprenticeships, get little or no training.

The distinction between the time-served craftsman and all other workers is more sharp in Britain than in any other industrial country. In 1976 the scheme rather clumsily named 'unified vocational preparation' was introduced on a pilot basis. Combining basic education with familiarizing young people with work in a group of related occupations, unified vocational preparation has now been adopted by the distribution industry's training board and by rubber and plastic processing. The preparation is fairly brief, like the Manpower Services Commission's short industrial training courses. But it is at least a move into this underdeveloped area.

Britain's backwardness in training and vocational education is made more serious by the mismatch of the existing skills of the labour force and the skills that will be in demand for the new technologies. The British training system, even though there has been rapid expansion in the last fifteen years, is still too limited to cope with the introduction of a whole generation to the new technologies. It is also too rigid to handle the retraining of people with obsolete skills and the updating of people's existing skills. Training is not glamorous. Little attention is paid to it by the media. Yet the inadequacy of the British training system is one of the greatest obstacles to the country's industrial regeneration.

GERMANY: APPRENTICESHIPS FOR EVERYONE

The Federal Republic of Germany offers a marked contrast. Training has been used in the Federal Republic for years both as a means of improving the knowledge and skills of the workforce and as a buffer against teenage unemployment. Young Germans, unless they are staying on in full-time education, must by law attend vocational schools for a minimum of eight hours a week after they leave school and until they reach the age of eighteen. The overwhelming majority of school-leavers, over 90 per cent, enter into a two- or three-year apprenticeship, which is an individual contract with an employer intended to provide on-the-job training in a given occupation. The young person qualifies by taking a series of tests and examinations. The regulations for each trade or industry are administered and regularly updated by the Federal

Institute of Vocational Education, on which employers and trade unions are both represented.

The system has its weaknesses. In some crafts and in some enterprises the quality of training is unimpressive, and monitoring is sketchy. Training allowances – and apprentices do not get wages – are set in a collective bargaining process and vary a good deal, traditional female occupations receiving the lowest rates. Furthermore, many apprentices qualify in occupations for which there is no demand. There are thousands of qualified butchers and bakers in the Federal Republic with little opportunity to practise their skills. The central tenet of the German apprenticeship system, however, is that a young man or woman trained for any occupation is better placed than one who is not trained at all. He or she will know something about how the economy works, will have acquired good working practices and will have the benefit of a solid vocational foundation.

In 1976, a basic full-time vocation year, the *Berufsgrundjahr* (BGJ) was introduced, both to meet the need for additional places and to broaden the occupational training of school-leavers. This foundation year has been controversial, largely because it is controlled by the education authorities, the Länder, and not by the employers. But it has given the German system the flexibility to deal with rising numbers of young people and the ability to place those who do not get apprenticeships in private firms.

The Federal Republic has consistently held youth unemployment down to 5 per cent or less. When, in 1973, youth unemployment became a serious problem in all OECD countries, it was the Federal Republic that came up with the most effective response. The Training Places Promotion Act of 1976 proposed a levy on firms if insufficient additional training places were offered to absorb the rising number of young people looking for them. The law has never had to be activated. Between 1975 and 1979, the number of apprenticeships available increased by 145,000 to 625,000. The policy was reinforced by the expansion of the *Berufsgrundjahr*, which took 67,000 young people in 1979/80, and parallel full-time courses directed at children with physical handicaps or low educational attainments. As for adaptation to the new technologies, the content of vocational and training courses is regularly reviewed to ensure it is up to date. Recently the metal trades moved over to a new form of apprenticeship, the cooperative year, interspersing blocks of vocational education with blocks of on-the-job training, and broadening each apprentice's experience of different metal-working skills.

The Federal government in 1980 offered 500 million Deutschmarks to subsidize 'in-house' training and retraining of existing employees in new processes, a proposal that was immediately taken up so enthusiastically by German enterprises that another 500 million Deutschmarks had to be found from pension funds to meet the demand. Partly because of this eagerness to maintain and improve 'human capital', the Federal Republic has attracted investment in processes requiring skilled labour. A virtuous circle has been established, in which the presence of skilled people acts as an engine for growth, and the growth in turn demands more skilled people. It is of course not the only element in the Federal Republic's economic success story, which includes effective co-determination at works level and responsive management, but it is a significant one.

A TRAINING SCHEME FOR BRITAIN

Part of the answer to the problem of unemployment, and particularly to youth unemployment, lies in creating such a virtuous circle. The Youth Opportunities Programme has shown the value of work experience together with training in social skills, as a bridge from school to work. We need now to move towards an ordered transition from school to work for all young people, as Albert Book and I proposed in February 1979. Work experience, the learning of social skills and basic vocational training should be available to every school-leaver, and wherever possible should be conducted partly on work premises, combining work experience with further education and training. Indeed, for many 'school-tired' young people, vocational courses combined with short periods of work experience in school holidays could usefully start in the fourth or fifth forms, at the age of fourteen or fifteen. By the end of the decade, every school-lever ought to be able to take a transitional course, perhaps called a traineeship. The length of the course might differ according to the amount of preparation required. Some traineeships could last two years, and lead on to technical qualifications. Others might be only six months long, similar to the current MSC short industrial courses or to unified vocational preparation. All such courses should include material to make young people familiar with the new technologies, what they are and what they can do. A national traineeship system, based on further education colleges, apprenticeship schools and work experience, could be complemented by a form of 'open college', television and radio programmes and video cassettes showing what the new technologies are about, what job opportunities they offer and what qualifications are needed.

Radio and television are not good means of instruction, but they are excellent stimulators of interest. Once interest has been stimulated, proper instructors and teaching materials, some specifically prepared for distance learning, have to take over. It is the combination of radio and television with traditional methods of education that is so powerful, as the successful adult literacy scheme demonstrated. Britain, with good broadcasting services, the experience of the Open University and an extensive further education system, is in a strong position to mount both a youth traineeship scheme and a national programme to make people aware of the new technologies. The fourth channel offers an opportunity to do it.

Britain needs more highly skilled people as well as more trainees. It should be possible to get some broad idea of requirements from firms themselves, from the industrial training boards and from the Training Services Division of the Manpower Services Commission. There are then three ways of meeting that need. The first is to construct a new apprenticeship system based on skill modules, encouraged if necessary by government subsidization of places. The industrial training boards should establish a broad foundation year, as the Engineering Industry Training Board has done. Such a year might be shared between further education colleges and approved training firms. School pupils who wanted to take an apprenticeship could be released for vocational courses to the local colleges for part of their final school year or years. The benefits of motivating young people who have lost interest in academic study would be considerable for the schools as well as for themselves.

Second, adult training and retraining should contribute to reducing unemployment and improving Britain's economic prospects. I have already mentioned the resistance adult trainees encounter at least in some occupations and in some parts of the country. There are other serious obstacles to the training of adults. Traditionally apprenticeships begin at sixteen, and apprentices' wages increase year by year. Yet there is no reason why apprenticeships should start at sixteen. Many boys and girls would benefit from an extra year or so at school, in which they could pick up additional O levels and CSEs, or even an A level, and would not be competing for scarce jobs. Apprenticeships ought to be open to any youngster up to eighteen; and indeed training after eighteen should be open too, though for adults allowances would have to be at least equivalent to the labourer's wage for that occupation. A more radical change would be to use standards of attainment rather than the passage of time as the requirement for completing an apprenticeship. Craftsmen and women should attain certain tough standards of skill and competence which might indeed normally require three or four years of experience and study. But it is the attainment of the standards that should protect craft status, not the passage of time. Many apprenticeships are too long; their length is maintained as a device for controlling entry. Given the legal safeguards that now exist for those already employed, control over entry should be made less rigid.

The third reform that is needed, if Britain is ever to realize the potential of her young people as Germany and Sweden do, is to introduce a system of training allowances and educational maintenance allowances for sixteen- to nineteen-year-olds. The young person should choose the most appropriate form of further education for him or her individually, whether it is staying on at school, an apprenticeship or a traineeship. The allowances up to the age of eighteen should be within the same range as supplementary benefit, with some flexibility to allow for the extra costs of travelling to work, tools, etc. To keep the cost down, it could at least initially be related to family income. Employers might contribute to the apprentice's allowance, but in the first two years the basic allowance should come from public funds. This would encourage expansion, and at a time of very high unemployment, the net cost to the Exchequer would not be high since the young people might otherwise be unemployed.

These three elements of a national training programme could help to transform Britain's economic prospects. It would take time, perhaps ten years from when such a programme was fully under way, to make a major impact. But even in the intervening years, the atmosphere among young people and unemployed people would be transformed. It deserves a high priority.

7

A Policy for Full Employment

THE DURATION OF WORK

There is a large family of ideas that come within the general definition of altering the duration of work over a week, a year or, more radically, a lifetime. The most often advocated is the shorter working week. It will contribute to the creation of jobs only if productivity does not rise to make good the loss of output and if overtime is not increased to compensate. For if overtime is so increased, the shorter working week becomes a device for obtaining higher wages, not for easing unemployment. There is another difficulty too. If earnings for the shorter week remain the same as they were for the original working week – and understandably unions usually demand this – then either the unit costs of labour will rise, pushing up the price of the product, or else productivity will increase and unit costs stay the same. Recent research indicates that a modest reduction in the working week in manufacturing enterprises of around 5 per cent has created no new jobs at all.[1] A more drastic approach would be to ban overtime; in Britain in September 1980 nearly ten million hours of overtime a week were being worked,[2] the equivalent of 250,000 jobs if no one had been allowed to work more than a forty-hour week. But practically any reduction in overtime depends on unions and employers agreeing on an earnings structure which raises the basic wage rate and reduces the overtime rate. Indeed, from the point of view of reducing unemployment, a single rate with no built-in incentive to overtime would be the ideal outcome. Another variant of this approach is the

Belgian ban on 'moonlighting' – second jobs for people with full-time jobs. However, as the word implies, 'moonlighting' jobs are hard to police; many of them are in the unofficial or 'private' economy.

A big reduction in overtime might create jobs. But in Britain the present structure of collective bargaining makes that outcome unlikely. Over and above whatever national bargains may be struck, British unions and employers engage in local or plant bargaining. Overtime rates, and the question of how much overtime is guaranteed, are usually dealt with at plant level. Management often prefers overtime to creating extra jobs, because extra jobs mean additional non-wage costs and substantial financial commitments of a permanent or semi-permanent kind. Shop stewards will fight for overtime because their members want it, and high overtime rates reinforce that demand. As in so many other instances in Britain, the answer is obvious, but the institutional and traditional obstacles to getting there are daunting.

Two attractive though marginal approaches to reducing the working year are longer holidays and more jobs with flexible hours. The first of these is beginning to gain ground in Britain, after a long period in which the country lagged far behind continental countries. The second offers a real chance to improve the quality of life and to create some additional jobs, especially for people with domestic responsibilities. 'Flexitime' allows people to choose their own hours, often around a core of three or four hours when everyone is expected to be present. Not only does it meet the needs of people who want to work five or six hours a day rather than eight, it also helps to create a more stable pattern of demand for public transport, shops and other amenities, so that people can avoid the stress of rush-hours or lunch-time shopping. And because people are paid for the hours they work, those who choose to do less than a full day's work leave room for other people to be employed.

Another set of proposals would reduce the length of working life. At one end, this can be done by extending education or training; for instance, by raising the school-leaving age, or by introducing a longer period of initial training before work (as suggested above) or by encouraging more young people to go on to higher education full time. At the other end of working life, voluntary early retirement schemes are being extended to more and more occupations. Such schemes have contributed substantially to reducing registered unemployment in Denmark, France and other continental European countries. However, if the voluntary retirement age is very young, say fifty or fifty-five as for firemen and policemen, it is virtually certain the person concerned will not actually retire: he or she will take a pension and get another job. This leads some people to advocate that early and final retirement from work should be compulsory. Obviously there are strong objections to such a policy on the grounds both of the need for wages to supplement state pensions and of people's individual right to choose whether they work or not. Furthermore, compulsory early retirement can cause real suffering to active, bored people – the so-called young elderly. Compulsory retirement is a two-edged weapon, which can produce its own nemesis, as the USA has found. Moves towards early retirement there led to a sharp reaction from a highly organized lobby, nicknamed 'grey power'. On 6 April 1978 Congress raised the statutory retirement age for most workers to seventy, with effect from 1 January 1979.

The duration of working life, rather than being shortened, can be made more intermittent – breaking it up into acts with intermissions, one might say. This is the idea of paid education leave or sabbaticals. It is not the same thing as retraining, which relates to the job or to a new job. It is, rather, the right of men and women after a given number of years of work to take a few months off, on basic pay, to broaden their education or, if they prefer, to improve their skills. Universities in the more affluent countries have long offered this attractive perk to the senior faculty, sometimes on the basis of one year's leave in seven, as the word sabbatical suggests. It is an idea that might well be more widely taken up in collective bargaining, so that people can enjoy education and time off when they are middle-aged as well as when they are young or retired.

A number of European countries, for instance France, have already adopted some form of paid education leave for certain professions and trades, and the practice is being extended. Like flexitime, its most significant contribution is towards improving the quality of people's lives during their working years. I do not want to exaggerate the contribution it can make towards reducing unemployment. But just as training schemes for young people delay entry into the labour market, paid education leave on a substantial scale could be a constructive alternative way of reducing the supply of labour and would provide additional jobs for teachers too. Much more than these proposals, however, will be required to return to full employment, or at least to the right to full employment, since there may indeed be young people who prefer intermittent work and leisure at least for a few years.

JOB CREATION

One approach to restoring full employment that should not be neglected is job creation. The United States has been remarkably successful in creating new jobs. Between 1975 and 1979 twelve million new jobs were created in both the public and private sectors, 90 per cent of them in the tertiary sector with an emphasis on information-related services. Many, indeed most, of the jobs in the private sector were in firms with under twenty employees. Job creation by government in the USA has been mainly through public works, and has been a feature of US counter-cyclical employment policy since the 1930s. Public service job creation is however hampered by very strict rules and regulations intended to prevent substitution. In those areas of the USA that are traditionally high wage areas these restrictions limit the efficiency of public works schemes.

European governments are much more ready to subsidize temporary or permanent jobs in the private sector than the USA is. Apart from its employment projects, which again are really public works schemes, Denmark pays employment subsidies for the long-term unemployed for up to a year. The Federal Republic subsidizes training places in private industry for handicapped and disadvantaged young people who cannot be easily placed, and the UK government has subsidized additional apprenticeships and sandwich places in industry. There is scope for increasing public works and subsidized employment projects as emergency measures for reducing youth unemployment. The Youth Conservation Corps in the USA and the community industry and work experience projects run by the UK Manpower Services Commission provide examples, ranging from afforestation and the clearing of rivers and canals to improving derelict neighbourhoods or insulating existing housing stocks. Such projects, however, especially when directed at unemployed young people, should include a training element, and should not be so short that the young person is given no adequate grounding for permanent employment. The 'make work' schemes of the inter-war depression are not an acceptable model. The combination of work experience with training is the key to helping young people to get jobs.

A determination to return to the option of full employment involves also a more radical questioning of the economic principles that have dominated the thinking and policy making of the industrialized countries for a very long time. These economic principles have been shared alike by market economies, mixed economies and command economies. There is no ideological distinction in the support they evince. They originate in the domination of human beings by the industrial process or, as Marx put it, the subordination of society to new modes of production. Karl Polanyi, in *The Great Transformation*, described how the Industrial Revolution improved the techniques of production while immiserating the lives of the people: 'the common sense attitude towards change', he wrote, 'was discarded in favour of a mystical readiness to accept the social consequences of economic improvement, whatever they might be'.[3]

The industrial economies are still creatures of that mystical readiness to accept the social consequences of economic improvement, even if that economic improvement entails unemployment and impoverished lives for millions of people. The argument for doing so is weakened when an adequate economic standard has been attained already. The argument for doing so is destroyed if one can show that the social consequences of economic improvement need not entail unemployment at all. We are slaves of our own traditional assumptions, of old ways of looking at the world.

The manufacturing countries have for generations tried to find ways of saving labour. They have substituted capital for labour, energy for labour and raw materials for labour. Large factories were constructed to allow expensive capital equipment to be used economically. The assembly line allowed for the maximum division of labour, at the cost of unsatisfactory working conditions and tediously repetitive work. Economies of scale encouraged companies to merge and grow into huge corporations, some of them multinational. None of these developments were about improving the quality of people's lives. They were about maximizing profit and minimizing the use of labour. We have been mesmerized into using the productivity of labour as the most important criterion of economic achievement.

The emphasis on substituting capital and raw materials for labour has also coloured the approach of the universities, polytechnics and technical colleges to the training of managers, accountants and engineers. Managers and engineers learn how to manage plant and machinery. Accountants learn how to manage company finance and company assets. But very few students of these subjects are taught how to work with other human beings. It is not surprising if men and women educated along these lines try to minimize the factor of labour as against the other factors of production. For labour is people, with their unpredictability, their moods and their wish to be consulted and informed. With the disappearance of the deferential, semi-educated generation born before the First World War, employing and therefore managing people has become even more demanding than it used to be.

The problems of managing people are made more acute in Western European countries, particularly in those as class-conscious as Britain, by the segregation of children during their school lives, either in academic schools as compared to general schools and vocational schools, or in fee-paying schools as compared to schools paid for by the state.

Many children of middle-class European families either attend private schools or are to be found only in the selective state schools, the lycées or the Gymnasiums. Consequently, friendships and peer groups are rarely formed across the social and class divide. The children of managers and professional people in turn become managers and professional people. The children of workers work for them. Each class is ignorant of the other, and sometimes apprehensive as well. The great achievement of the American high school was the destruction of social barriers; the school was the school of the entire community. As the children grew up, they were able to work together and play together and measure each other not by inherited status but by present achievement. Western Europe has not so far attained that kind of social fluidity. The social gulfs in Western Europe add to the strains and tensions of managing people.

MORE JOBS, FEWER MATERIALS

Yet it is in looking afresh at the use of people as compared to capital, energy and raw materials that we may find a route back to full employment. For what matters in measuring the efficient use of resources is not just the productivity of labour, but the productivity of all the factors of production combined: labour, capital, land, energy, raw materials and knowledge. It will of course be argued that the productivity of labour is the key to a country's ability to compete for trade and for markets. I do not dispute that men and women should be employed efficiently. Poor management, inadequate information about what people are supposed to be doing, and badly synchronized flows of raw materials, components and deliveries to markets reduce labour productivity. So do trade union restrictive practices, both in the professions and the trade unions; in certain industries such as the notorious London newspaper industry they have become suicidal. Inadequate training is another reason for low productivity. The list is long. The argument that follows is not an argument for believing that low labour productivity is a good thing. It is an argument for saying that our mix of factors of production is heavily influenced by our bias against employing people rather than machines, and against conserving energy and raw materials if it is necessary to increase the number of jobs in order to do so.

The choices between factors of production, and the substitution of one for another, are influenced by fiscal and taxation policies which build in a cost preference against labour, not least the add-on costs of social security. They are also influenced by psychological attitudes. There is the subtle effect of using not the productivity of all the factors but of one only, labour, as our measure of efficiency. It is not, for instance, clear in a world short of land and long on people that economic achievement in agriculture should be measured in terms of productivity per man rather than productivity per hectare.

Energy, land and raw materials have all become more expensive and more scarce, not just absolutely more expensive but also relatively more expensive. Energy costs, for instance, have recently gone up faster than the general rate of inflation, and faster than earnings. Therefore a fresh assessment of the mixture of factors of production is required, and that fresh assessment must break with traditional attitudes.

Over a wide area, labour can be substituted for capital or capital for labour without affecting overall costs of production. Indeed, in some cases costs of production may be reduced by substituting labour for capital. There is evidence to show that capital-intensive processes have been introduced into, and used in, Third World countries despite the availability of many unemployed workers. Many managers trained in the industrialized world's universities and colleges simply don't know how to organize substantial labour forces, so they use machinery instead. An arresting example of this appeared in Andrew Shonfield's book, *The Attack on World Poverty*, in which he described the contrast between building a dam in India and building a dam in China.[4] The Indian dam was built by sophisticated imported machinery and employed only a handful of people; its construction was watched by the hungry and unemployed local people. In China, the local people would build the dam, moving hundreds of tons of earth in wheelbarrows and baskets, and being paid a living wage to do it. Even in such extreme cases of labour available at low cost; Western-trained managers were disinclined to employ large numbers of people.

Small firms are usually more labour-intensive than big ones; indeed the whole net increase in jobs in the United States since 1967 (fifteen million of them) has come from small firms. Communication between managers and workers is easier and more informal in a small enterprise. The human problems are on a scale that can be dealt with by readily available management and trade union skills. Large firms are inclined to substitute capital for labour. In Britain between 1970 and 1977, firms with over five hundred employees had a net loss of 842,000 jobs; medium-sized firms showed an increase of 797,000; and small firms with under a hundred employees, an increase of 243,000. In the United States workforces of large firms have declined.

There have not been many studies of alternative mixes of factors of production to get the best result for society as a whole, no doubt because labour productivity has been unquestioned as the measure of efficiency. But here and there some provocative findings have emerged. In July 1976 a group of independent experts produced a report for the Social Affairs Directorate of the European Commission.[5] The experts warned of the danger that European Community countries might settle for 'an economic equilibrium of under-employment', a perceptive warning as it turned out. They recommended the elimination of obstacles to geographic and occupational mobility and measures to improve the quality of labour, including training. They advocated effective placement services and vocational guidance. But then they looked at the ways in which the demand for labour might be improved. 'The time now seems ripe', they said, 'to question the general preference given to investment aids at the expense of employment subsidies.'

The group pointed out that in the twenty years from 1950 to 1971 gross fixed capital formation increased as a proportion of gross national product in every Community member country. Yet studies in some European countries, particularly France, showed a decline in the value added per unit of capital employed. In Britain, returns to the highly capitalized large bakers are low, while overhead and transportation costs are high. Other industries, like pottery and furniture, which in the past were based on small enterprises using skilled workpeople, may not have improved their efficiency in terms of added value by becoming more capital intensive. Ill-judged or inefficient investment adds to inflation. The experts questioned the purposes of investment: 'Have they (investment projects) not been directed more towards the productivity of labour (and the displacing of jobs) than towards the total productivity of the factors of production?' Answering their own question, the experts proposed that investment for expansion be distinguished from investment for rationalization. The latter, they pointed out, can destroy more jobs than it saves.

HUMAN ASSETS

John Davis, consultant to the Intermediate Technology Development Group in Britain, pursued a similar train of thought

in a seminal article published in *Accountancy Age* in April 1978.
'Productivity is really only improved', he wrote,

if the combination of manpower costs and capital investment costs are
reduced for each unit of 'added value' created. There is no point in
reducing the manpower cost element by increasing output per employee if
it can only be achieved at an increased cost of investment that is bigger than
the manpower cost saving. Overall productivity is increased only if the
utilization of all resources, men, money and material, is improved.

Given the high cost of capital in Britain, and the relatively low
cost of labour, Davis demonstrated that a Japanese pattern of high
capital intensity and low use of manpower applied to Britain would
consume more resources overall, and therefore be more expensive
than the existing British pattern for each additional £1m of added
value. Minimizing manpower cost does not necessarily correspond
with the optimum use of all resources. Davis gives a further example
of a company that improved its working methods substantially
without a significant increase in investment. The average return on
capital employed rose to 30 per cent, well above the estimated
return if the path of high capital investment and a reduction in the
workforce had been followed. These comparisons are, of course, based
on the costs to the company alone. If the social costs of unemployment are added in, the comparisons become even more telling.

Accountancy practices reinforce the tendency of business
enterprises to favour capital in any mixture of factors of production.
Capital spent on buildings or equipment goes down in a company's
books as assets. Any modernization or improvement increases the
assets and also the security against which the company can borrow
money. Nothing appears in a company's accounts in relation to its
workforce. If the quality of the workforce is improved, by training
or retraining in new skills, the company's assets do not increase in
any way, even though the more highly skilled workforce is clearly
more valuable. Labour, it may be argued, is free to quit the
company; machines can't go away. But just as depreciation is
applied to the value of plant and equipment, so an allowance for
turnover or wastage can be applied to labour. A firm which retains
its workers by good management and good working conditions will

suffer a lower labour depreciation than a firm with high turnover. It is certainly not beyond the wit of accountants to value human assets as well as capital assets, and it would remove yet another significant distortion in comparing factor costs.

In the autumn of 1970, the Institute of Personnel Management and the Institute of Cost and Management Accountants established a working party on human asset accounting. In October 1972 W. J. Giles and D. Robinson published a study, *Human Asset Accounting*, based on the working group's findings. The authors found that training was almost invariably treated as a cost or overhead in articles and pamphlets on the subject. No attention at all was given to the idea that people are assets to their organizations and that the assets can appreciate through training. Yet only if human beings are seen as an asset to their company rather than merely as an expense can managers 'make meaningful choices between various types of human investment, between human investment and investment in other assets, and in addition give due consideration to an adequate return on those assets'.[6] Rensis Likert, in a book called *The Human Organization: its Management and Value*,[7] proposed that a major portion of training costs should be treated as capital investment and its cost be depreciated accordingly. The working party was told of an experiment in a human resource accounting system by the R. G. Barry Corporation of Columbus, Ohio. The corporation found that the new system not only provided a truer picture of its performance; it also transformed the attitude of management towards training, good industrial relations and wastage.

The working party was attracted by the idea of human asset accounting and worked out detailed conventions for accounting purposes. Accountants already distinguish between the break-up value of a company's assets and its much greater value as a going concern. The difference between the two provides a rough measure of the value of the company's human resources. The working party found that human resources could be assessed much more precisely than that. The report's authors believed that benefits in allocation of resources, industrial relations, training and development would flow from human asset accounting. But they went further:

The whole idea of human asset accounting seems in keeping with the times, countering the advance of technology which so often appears to result in a devaluing of men's contribution to enterprise. If the workforce sees itself recognized as a vital asset of its organization, much of its dignity will be restored. In turn, if management viewed the workforce as an asset rather than an expense, its attitude could somersault from constraining and demanding to conserving and developing.[8]

Labour and capital are not the only factors of production that can be substituted for one another. Labour, as pointed out above, can also be substituted for land or for raw materials. The rehabilitation of existing houses and neighbourhoods is more labour-intensive than pulling them down and rebuilding by industrialized methods. But it makes fewer demands on land. Agriculture provides an even better example. Intensively farmed land, such as gardens, smallholdings, allotments and fish farms, has a very high yield per acre and lower labour productivity compared to extensively farmed land. If land is scarce and labour is plentiful, agricultural methods can be changed to allow for that new balance. Modern agriculture is energy-intensive, but it need not be. Methods of organic farming make far fewer demands on fuel and fertilizer, but more demands on labour.

In the use of energy, inputs of labour and prime fuel are to some extent interchangeable. District heating schemes that use low-grade fuels and domestic rubbish are more labour-intensive than big generating stations supplying electricity for both lighting and heating. Furthermore, the big generating stations use prime fuel; supplying space-heating demand from electricity generated in this way is an expensive and highly inefficient use of energy. Much of that energy goes into heating poorly insulated or uninsulated houses. A very large proportion of the existing housing stock in Western Europe is inadequately insulated. To build new houses to a high standard of energy conservation requires more labour initially in construction than the average house, but produces such a substantial saving in energy bills that the extra cost can be amortized within three or four years. Using unemployed men and women to insulate existing buildings could absorb thousands of people in semi-skilled and unskilled jobs, and also produce substantial savings for the nation in terms of lower energy bills – savings that would grow in value as energy costs go on rising faster than the general level of inflation. A national insulation programme would be self-financing, and could contribute substantially towards reducing unemployment.

There are many other examples. Long-life products such as consumer durables and motorcars need very little additional input of raw materials or energy compared to short-life products, but require more careful design and better workmanship. Maintaining and repairing them make greater demands on labour, in particular on skilled labour, than scrapping and replacing. The work involved is also much more satisfying than work on a factory assembly line. The marketing of goods can also use more labour and less raw material; for instance, home delivery or good after-sales service can be as effective selling methods as attractive packaging.

GOVERNMENTS MAKE JOBS EXPENSIVE

There are implications in all these ideas for government policy. I have referred earlier to the urgent need for more resources for training and retraining, though the cost could be limited by mobilizing existing assets in education, industry and broadcasting. Employment would be encouraged by changes in the tax system which could be financially neutral; it is a matter of the balance between taxes and allowances affecting the relative cost of labour, capital and other factors. In a growing economy, the capital available to each worker is normally increased in order to enable him to produce a higher added value. But, as the group of independent experts said in their European Commission report:

The granting of interest rate subsidies, tax relief in respect of depreciation, and investment aids, regional or others, lowers the cost of using capital. Furthermore, the use of wages as the base for social security contributions and certain parafiscal charges leads to changes in the parameters within which the employer makes his calculations and tends to accelerate the substitution of capital for labour.

Non-wage costs of labour continue to grow as social security contributions increase and as occupational pensions and company health schemes are more widely introduced. In many Western

European countries non-wage costs are now as much as 70 per cent of wage costs. The marginal cost of employing an additional person has therefore become much greater than the wages he or she earns. On top of that, the cost of training him or her is an additional expense to the company, which cannot be depreciated like a capital investment. (In the Federal Republic of Germany, firms can write off their training costs against revenues for tax purposes: it is an important incentive.) A serious attempt to restore full employment, therefore, would involve a review of tax incentives and tax allowances for capital investment, at least distinguishing between capital investment that produces a net growth of jobs and capital investment which destroys jobs. It would mean reconsidering the shift of social security and health costs from general tax revenues to payroll taxes, for that is what has been happening in recent years. Social security and health costs could be met by a levy on turnover rather than on wages and salaries alone. Another proposal worth exploring is the waiving of an employer's national insurance payments for a period after he recruits an additional young person, as is done in Italy. Even more innovative, a recent French law allows workers to draw six months' unemployment benefit in advance in order to finance new job opportunities for themselves. Seven thousand new small enterprises have been launched on this basis since the law was passed in 1979.[9]

Re-examining our assumptions about the use of labour would have repercussions for courses in management studies, engineering and design. The responsibilities of enterprises to the local community and to their employees would be emphasized. Management of people would become a much larger part of these courses. Engineers and designers would learn to think more about the makers and users of their products. They would learn to minimize the need for energy and they would avoid wasting raw materials, even though the design might be less simple and might need longer to make.

In the fourth Rita Hinden Memorial Lecture, entitled 'Technology and Political Change', given on 17 January 1976, Dr E. F. Schumacher declared: 'Once a process of technological development has been set in motion, it proceeds largely by its own momentum irrespective of the intentions of its originators. It demands an appropriate "system", for inappropriate systems spell inefficiency and failure.'

The process of substituting the other factors of production for labour has its own momentum and has created a system of presumptions which few people appear to question. Yet there is no inevitability about it. Human beings should control economic systems, though historically the opposite has more often been true. There is no reason why the industrialized countries should drift towards mass unemployment. Yet that is the way some of them are going, including Britain. If governments respond too late, then firms and unions will be driven into the Canute-like postures of defending jobs however unviable or obsolete, fighting losing battles to prevent redundancies, even occupying plants, and finally being undermined by people who are weary of the battle and prefer to accept the apparently generous redundancy money they are offered. It is not necessary, if only the deep conservatism of governments, firms and unions can be overcome.

8

Less Concentration: Industry

The prospects for future employment can be greatly improved by measures of the kind described in the last chapter. So can the long-term prospects for the British economy. But in the next five years, employment and living standards depend upon the present British economy's capacity to sustain output and its share of the world market.

In the mid-1980s, the underlying weaknesses of that economy will be partly obscured by revenues from North Sea oil, expected to amount to £10,000 million in 1982/3 and £15,000 million in 1984/5 (at 1978/9 prices, £2.75 billion and £4.25 billion respectively). North Sea oil is an ambiguous blessing. It makes a major contribution to the balance of payments, but it also drives up the value of the pound in international money markets, making it harder to sell other British exports abroad.

North Sea oil apart, it has become the contemporary fashion to regard British manufacturing industry as a disaster area, badly managed, plagued by strikes, offering products that are poorly designed and unimaginatively marketed. The British are their own worst salesmen, as any cursory reading of the newspapers demonstrates. Lack of confidence within the country inspires lack of confidence outside; and that lack of confidence has a real cost in terms of orders not won, products not sold and jobs not saved.

The facts, as distinct from the image, show that British manufacturing industry is a curate's egg, a mixture of the very good, the very bad and of many enterprises in the middle. The range from good to bad is probably wider than in many other countries for the good are among the world leaders in their field, in design, production methods, industrial relations and technical innovation, while the bad are bad in almost every respect.

British performance in the European Community is sometimes offered as an illustration of the country's inability to compete. It shows nothing of the kind. Measured in Deutschmarks, a stable currency, the value of British exports to the European Community grew at an average rate of 16.8 per cent per annum between 1972 and 1979, and to the rest of the world by 8.6 per cent per annum. This was, of course, before North Sea oil became a significant factor in the UK balance of trade. Imports rose too, but by less: by 16.4 per cent per annum from the European Community over the same period, and from the rest of the world by 8.4 per cent per annum.[1] UK manufacturing exports are often singled out as an area of particular weakness. Yet if UK manufactures had grown at the same rate as world exports between 1972 and 1976, then the ratio of 1976 to 1972 would be unity – 1:0. In fact the ratio for British exports to the European Community was 1.34 between those years, and for the rest of the world 0.76. Between 1976 and 1977 the ratio for exports to the Community was 2.16, for the rest of the world 1.47.[2] Using a different criterion, that of increase in the volume of exports, then again the British export performance between 1970 and 1978 was not far out of line with the West German achievement. British export volume grew 58 per cent in those eight years, West German 67 per cent.

Of those who contributed to this creditable performance, some industries were much better than others. Chemicals, furniture, food, drink and tobacco, electrical engineering and metal manufactures all improved exports relative to imports. Vehicles, textiles, clothing and footwear all saw imports increase much more than exports. Yet even these less successful industrial sectors had great differences within them. In vehicles, Ford UK held its share of domestic and export markets. In clothing and footwear, the fashion sector and woollens did well. It is the textile industry, still going through a painful process of adjustment to competition from newly industrializing countries, and British Leyland, which looms so large in manufacturing employment, that have dragged down Britain's economic performance.

Nor was British industry particularly unprofitable until it was hit by a combination of an overvalued pound and high interest rates in 1980, though the profits of manufacturing were below those of other sectors. The Bank of England estimates that the pre-tax rate of return on the capital of industrial and commercial companies was over 8 per cent in 1977 and 1978, compared to 11.5 per cent in the 1960s when taxes on companies were much higher. Industry's profits in money terms rose from £7,000 million in 1974 to £16,000 million in 1978, holding nearly steady at £15,000 million in 1979; in real terms, therefore, profits were fairly stable over those five years. But profits are expected to fall to £10,000 million in 1981 as the recession and the over-valued pound combine to batter them. In real terms, 1981 profits will be less than half of what they were in 1979.[3] Again, British firms have widely different levels of profitability, measured as return on assets. Of Europe's thousand largest industrial companies, in 1978 only sixteen had a return on assets exceeding 20 per cent; nine of those sixteen were British-based companies, including one, British Aerospace, in public ownership.[4]

PERFORMANCE

The responsibility for the poor performance of parts of British industry is often laid at the door of the trade unions. Undoubtedly there are extensive restrictive practices in British industry, resistance to the introduction of new methods and often strained industrial relations. But the much better performance, at least until the 1970s, of US subsidiaries in Britain than of British-run companies suggests that British management has a good deal to answer for too. US subsidiaries, according to Professor John Dunning, earned higher rates of return on capital, had higher labour productivity, exported a larger proportion of their output, expanded more rapidly and paid higher wages in almost every industrial sector in which they operated than their British opposite numbers.[5] Professor Dunning's comparisons were based on results in 1970/71, and his more recent work shows that the profitability gap has narrowed considerably. British management is also becoming more technologically aware, though it is less highly trained and qualified than American management. The relatively new business schools in Britain have not yet had time to make much impact. The predominance of the graduates of one business school, Harvard, in the senior positions in US industry is almost as significant as the predominance of Oxford and Cambridge graduates in the British civil service. Two thirds of outside entrants to the administrative trainee grade in 1979/80 had Oxford or Cambridge degrees. So had over half of those in the three most senior ranks of the service in 1979.

Older British managers are often unresponsive to technological developments and to new trends in marketing. Recent evidence of the brake that non-technically-minded managers can impose on industrial development comes from the Policy Studies Institute's study on the applications of microprocessors to British manufacturing industry. The study found little evidence of trade union resistance. 'While none of the firms seems particularly worried about labour troubles,' said the report,

several speak of internal opposition in the boardroom itself . . . Some people even rate ignorance and opposition at the top as the most important single factor holding up progress, and draw a contrast with the competitor firms on the Continent which, they claim, are more often directed by people with a technical background rather than a financial one, with the result, they suggest, that they are more inclined to take an informed, positive and long-term attitude to technical innovation of all kinds.[6]

Employers and managers have been resistant not only to technical innovation but also to organizational change. Consultation with employees in many firms is episodic and inadequate. Shared decision-making is limited to a handful of pioneering firms. Organizations representing industry argue that the attitude of the trade unions makes a widespread adoption of worker participation risky: trade union members, they claim, are not committed to the success of the firm. It is a 'Catch 22' situation; for workpeople who are neither consulted nor informed are unlikely to be cooperative or even to know what the firm's objectives are. The union structure in Britain, where several unions may represent different groups of workers in the same enterprise, is not as conducive to industrial democracy as the industrial unionism of West Germany or Scandinavia, and that is particularly true of worker representation on the board, the proposal favoured in the Bullock Report. Even given that difficulty, however, progress has been notably slow. Disputes often occur as a result of a failure of communication; and the disputes themselves may take a long time to resolve, owing to complicated and sometimes prolonged grievance procedures. I shall have more to say about union attitudes in the next chapter. In this one, I would add that the fact that such a small proportion of British managers and employers have actually been through management training, and that so many have a financial or accounting background with little or no experience of organizing or managing human beings, is one of the root causes of Britain's poor industrial relations. Many directors still look upon the personnel managers or the directors responsible for industrial relations as lesser breeds; yet between a third and a half of management time in many companies is spent on human relations problems. Every dispute or stoppage of work costs money, sometimes running into millions of pounds.

British industry, whether good or bad, has shown a strong tendency towards concentration. The economies of scale have long been a significant theme of economists, and that theme has been reinforced by the high capital cost of much modern technology. Indeed it has been so expensive to start up in some sectors of industry that existing firms are in practice protected from competition. The assembly line and the multi-megawatt power station are both culminations of such technologies, involving the maximum division of labour in the first case and very high capital per person employed in the second. The story of modern industrial society has been the story of concentration into larger and larger groups and plants, finally leading to the multinational company with a turnover greater than the national product of some smaller countries.

Surprisingly few studies of concentration have been done, and those that there are provide an unsatisfactory basis for international comparison, owing to different statistical definitions of small, medium and large companies in different countries. There is no standardized international system for collecting such data, and even the definitions of establishments and enterprises vary. However, subject to these reservations, some broad conclusions can be reached.

THE SMALL ENTERPRISE

In the OECD area, small and medium-sized enterprises in manufacturing industry – that is to say enterprises with less than 500 employees – accounted for between 40 per cent and 70 per cent of all industrial employment, depending upon which OECD country one looked at, in 1977/8. The lowest proportions, 40–45 per cent, were in countries of medium size with a long industrial history – Britain, France and Germany. The highest proportions were in countries with small home markets: Switzerland, Denmark, Belgium, Canada and Australia.[7] The share of production accounted for by these enterprises was smaller than their share of employment, that is to say they were more labour intensive, or less labour productive, than big firms. They are now almost the only firms offering new industrial jobs; their share of total employment in manufacturing has increased in some countries. Indeed small firms in many OECD countries are weathering the recession better than large ones, though in the period between the end of the Second World War and 1973 they lost ground. In the decade from 1963 to 1973, the growth of large firms and the movement of successful medium-sized companies into the category of large firms seriously eroded the small and medium-sized group. The one major exception was the United States. The American domestic market is so large that innovative and enterprising companies, however small, can quickly make a mark if they have an attractive product.

Smaller firms generally have a good record of innovation; most successful large firms started as innovative small ones. According to Christopher Freeman's report to the Bolton Committee[8] small firms have made significant contributions to industries where there are many small suppliers – for example, electronics, scientific instruments and textile machinery – but not to process industries where few manufactured components are required – for example, steel, pharmaceuticals, aluminium, glass or cement. An American study[9] has shown that new firms start with product innovation and then, as they become larger and more established, move on to process innovation, having standardized their products. As competition ceases to be about performance and design, but turns rather on price and the minimization of cost, successful firms become larger, more hierarchical and less flexible in their operation. Another. American study shows how dramatic the growth of employment has been in firms embarking on new technologies compared with 'mature' companies, though admittedly the sample is small. The researchers compared five relatively small, new companies involved in 'young technology', five established companies with a good record of innovation, and six very large mature companies over the period 1969 to 1974. The 'young technology' companies had an annual growth rate of 40.7 per cent, and increased the number of people they employed by 552 per cent over the period; the established innovative companies grew at an annual rate of 4.3 per cent, and increased employment by 23 per cent; and the mature companies only managed to grow 0.6 per cent a year on average, and increased employment by 3 per cent in the five years.[10]

The enterprising and innovative characteristics of small firms and even more of new small firms in the United States is undeniable. Research, now rather out-of-date, on the major inventions of the twentieth century, and in particular of the decade after the war, showed that between half and two thirds had originated from small firms or independent inventors.[11] A more recent study[12] undertaken for the National Science Board of the United States attributes 47 per cent of major innovations in the period from 1953 to 1973 to firms employing under 1,000 employees, and 23 per cent to firms employing under 100. Small enterprise has an incredibly high birth rate in the USA, and quite a high mortality rate too. In every year from 1972 to 1976, over 300,000 companies were formed in the USA, and in every year about 10,000 were dissolved. The survivors were important sources of jobs.

In spite of the constraints on finance of a cautious and conventional banking sector, Britain too has a high company birth rate, averaging over 50,000 a year between 1972 and 1978, though I suspect many more were formed for taxation reasons or in the property and construction sector than in manufacturing. The mortality rate was dramatically higher than in the United States. In every year except 1978, dissolutions ran at half to two thirds the number of new company formations.[13]

CONCENTRATION

Despite this evidence of initiative among small businessmen, Britain is dominated by very large companies – over 5,000 employees – to a greater extent than any other industrial country and very much more so than the United States. Of Western Europe's 500 largest companies, 116 are based in Britain, a figure approached by no other European country except West Germany, which has 142.[14] Much neoclassical economic theory would suggest that the concentration of industry in Britain should give the country marked advantages; economies of scale, resources for capital investment and research and development. But the truth is different. Like so much economic theory, the argument for economies of scale leaves out the human factor. Large companies, whether publicly or privately owned, present quite special problems to management. Communications often become difficult and industrial relations strained in very large plants; most strikes take place in them, not in small or medium-sized firms. The layers of shop stewards, foremen and line managers between the shop floor and the senior management mean that the consultation and grievance processes are formalized and often ponderous. Furthermore, the manager of a very large enterprise has to be not just 'a bit better' than the manager of a small company; he needs to be a different kind of person, requiring exceptional administrative ability. The same is true of the head of a large school, compared to the head of a small school, or of the manager of a large hospital, compared to the manager of a small hospital. One of the reasons for education ministers in Britain adopting a de facto limit on the size of secondary schools of about 1,500 pupils was that the attributes that went to make a good teacher would be the attributes needed to be a good head teacher in a medium-sized school; but when a school has 2,000 pupils or more, it doesn't need a good teacher; it needs a manager, and that is an altogether different thing.

British governments have not tried to prevent the concentration of manufacturing and services in very large firms, nor have they done much to encourage small-scale enterprise, whether in the public or private sector. On the whole 'big is beautiful' has not been challenged. British monopoly and anti-trust legislation is weak, and whenever a large and powerful employer or a company in a poor region falls within the ambit of the Monopolies and Mergers Commission, governments tend to waive their own rules and exercise discretion in that company's favour. Between 1955 and 1969 there was a rash of mergers, in the years after 1965 often encouraged and even brought about by the Industrial Reconstruction Corporation (IRC) established by the first Wilson government. The Conservative government of 1970–74 pursued a similar course. Takeovers and mergers were encouraged, many of them forced through by buccaneering finance companies like Slater Walker, and by 'company doctors', some of them no more than thinly disguised asset-strippers. Indeed in those years many solid firms with good employment records and much customer goodwill went to the wall because they had assets that could be taken over and realized for large, once-for-all capital gains. The Labour government of 1974 brought the stampede of takeovers and asset-stripping under control; yet it retained a soft spot for concentration. In 1976, after a fierce Cabinet debate, Tate and Lyle, a substantial contributor of funds to the Conservative Party, was allowed to establish a virtual monopoly in sugar refining by taking over the efficient and innovative firm of Manbré and Garton, which resisted to the last. It is perhaps worth adding, for the benefit of those who believe that Labour governments invariably conspire with big capitalist corporations, that the argument that won the day with the Cabinet was the possibility of hundreds of redundancies in the sugar-cane refining industry if the takeover was not allowed to go through.

British governments have generally looked benevolently on mergers and even monopolies. Between 1965 and 1978 there were nearly 11,000 mergers of industrial, commercial and financial companies in Britain. Of these, only forty-three were referred to the Monopolies and Mergers Commission, which found thirteen to be against the public interest. As the 1978 Green Paper put it, 'The legislation has been framed on the assumption that most mergers are beneficial to the economy and that only a small minority warrant full investigation to assess whether, on balance, they are detrimental.' Yet a substantial majority of firms showed lower profits after a merger than before.[15]

The acceptance, even promotion, of concentrations in British industry has not been limited to the private sector. Socialists themselves long supported concentration in the public sector. Familiar with the great private corporations of the twentieth century industrial scene, the Labour party and its Fabian advisers produced their mirror-image in the Morrisonian public corporation, whose first exemplar was the London Passenger Transport Board. Alternative approaches to public ownership, such as publicly owned firms competing with private firms, state holdings of a proportion of a company's equity, industrial cooperatives, community and local enterprises have all been neglected. The British political parties moved down the road of concentration together, though each argued that the roads were different, because one ended in large public corporations and the other in large private ones.

THE PUBLIC SECTOR

Large corporations resemble one another in many ways, whether they are formally owned by private shareholders or by the state. The public sector in Britain, like the private sector, has been remarkable for the sheer size of many of its firms. A report by the Advisory Council for Applied Research and Development commented,

It is perhaps not fully appreciated that, compared with other countries, the United Kingdom is remarkable for the size and centralization of many of its utilities and public services. Our public corporations are often much larger than their counterparts in West Germany or even the USA; the CEGB [Central Electricity Generating Board] operates the largest integrated electricity supply system in the world, the NCB [National Coal Board] produces more deep-mined coal than any other single organization, and so on.

The report went on to criticize the imbalance in technical resources and therefore in research and development capacity between these large public corporations and the many small private sector suppliers, and reached a disturbing conclusion:

The substantial in-house R and D capabilities of public sector purchasing organizations – established for the best of reasons to promote the development of their industries and thereby to provide a better public service – have in our view resulted in a weakening of the technical base of United Kingdom manufacturing industry.[16]

British publicly owned corporations, like British privately owned ones, are well represented among Europe's biggest. Of the 116 British industrial companies in Europe's top 500, eleven are publicly owned – and this list does not include service companies like British Rail or British Airways, both also the largest in their respective sectors.[17]

Britain not only has a more highly concentrated manufacturing industry than her European and American competitors, but concentration has markedly intensified. In 1953, the hundred largest British manufacturing enterprises had a 27 per cent share of UK manufacturing net output; by 1972, the share had risen to 41 per cent.[18] In 1976, over twice as many British as German firms had a turnover of £640 millions or more, the figure then used by the European Community as the basis of merger control.[19] If the arguments for economies of scale were as strong as has been asserted in some financial and City quarters, it is hard to explain why British manufacturing is not markedly more cost-efficient than German or American manufacturing.

The history of natural selection tells us that size is irrelevant to survival. What matters is functional efficiency. The dinosaur proved to be an evolutionary dead end; the fish and the bird survived and flourished. Is it not possible that the passion for size accounts for part, at least, of our industrial plight, and for some of the rigidities of administered markets and administered pricing that add to inflationary pressures? Big business, like big labour, introduces an inflationary bias into the economy, because administered prices, like negotiated wages, are 'sticky downwards' even when demand falls.

Business practices, like past governments' policies, also lean towards the large firm. Big firms can get discounts from those who supply them, because they offer an assured market. They, in turn, can give discounts to their regular customers; one of the ways the big bakers, for instance, maintain their position is by offering retailers much larger discounts than smaller bakers can afford. Purchasing by public corporations is usually directed to large suppliers, reinforcing the trend to bigness. The National Coal Board, influenced by E. F. Schumacher, who worked there, once considered the idea of deliberately setting aside part of its purchases to encourage small suppliers, an idea that could be usefully emulated by other national industries but has not been. Advertising, especially where it is directed towards building up brand loyalties, similarly favours size, especially where distribution is highly organized and markets for many products are national rather than local. Britain's distributive trade is far more concentrated than that of any other European country except Finland, with nearly 54 per cent in the hands of multiple chains.[20] All these practices favour the large over the small.

A similar bias is found in financial markets, according to the 1980 Wilson Report on the City and financial institutions. 'There is no doubt that, compared to large firms, small firms are at a considerable disadvantage in financial markets. Loans are more expensive and security requirements are generally more stringent. External equity is more difficult to find and may only be obtainable on relatively unfavourable terms. Venture capital is particularly hard to obtain.'[21] The report goes on to point out that some government-financed support schemes and some export credit facilities exclude small firms altogether. Nor does the tax system do anything to redress the balance. Small and medium-sized businesses carry a proportionately heavier incidence of taxation than firms large enough to be liable to corporation tax, and they can rarely afford clever accountants to tell them how to reduce the burden.

The OECD studies, mentioned above, suggest that a period of slow or stable growth is not a bad climate for small firms, and that in the OECD area generally their position has improved or held steady since 1973. But a profound recession engineered in part by high interest rates is another matter altogether. In Professor Galbraith's words, 'The effect of tight money is very discriminating. It falls on the small man and largely exempts the large man.'[22] Any small firm that is driven to the banks or the financial markets for working capital – and in the current recession many have been – will almost certainly pay higher interest rates than a well-established large firm, if it can get money at all. Small firms also suffer dispropor-tionately from delays in paying money owing to them; few are in a position to finance extended credit.

Small firms are also at a disadvantage in that they lack the means to be mobile. The high cost of land and the unattractive surround-ings in big cities diverted many of the big factories and offices to the suburbs, to industrial parks and industrial zones of new towns. The cities themselves, which developed fast at the earlier stages of industrialization when the specialization of labour and the massive exchange of goods first became characteristic of the economy, began to shrink; some had to deal with dereliction. The jobs ebbed away, and with them the most enterprising young people. Local markets started to shrink. Many small firms collapsed, unable to pay rising rates and property taxes, yet without the resources or finance to make a move to a new location.

The new technologies, however, may prove a boon for small enterprises. Microprocessors can provide automatic and semi-automatic processes for small firms engaged in short runs or batch production. The machine tool becomes highly adaptable, so that the firm does not have to retool for every change in the specifi-cation. Furthermore, microelectronic devices are bringing down the costs of measurement, control and inspection, which have hitherto been major obstacles to the automation of small and medium-sized manufacturing companies. Computer-aided design opens up great possibilities for meeting customers' requirements for small quantities or even for individual products; the craft firm and the bespoke producer can regain their old positions. Everything will depend on the creativity and vigour of the particular firm, rather than on its size; or at least, it would, if other things were equal.

But of course they are not. The PSI study on the application of microelectronics to certain manufacturing industries showed that two of the five industries, physical test instruments and toys, had responded reasonably well to the opportunities offered by micro-electronics and were certainly aware of them, both being industries in which small firms predominate. But the smaller firms had to pay more for their chips, got less help from the chip manufacturers with developing applications, and found it harder to get the most up-to-date chips compared to large-volume manufacturers.[23] And even though the chips themselves are cheap, many existing products will have to be re-designed to make use of them, involving substantial costs for smaller firms.

What can be done to help them? For the argument of this chapter is that more small and medium-sized enterprises would help Britain to create more jobs, and would encourage product innovation. They would also mitigate the inflationary pressures inherent in corporatism, which have been so difficult to control.

The Wilson Committee jibbed at setting up a Small Business Agency, though the case for it seems strong. What the Committee did propose was a loan guarantee scheme, under which loans to small businesses would be partially underwritten by the banks, and an English Development Agency with similar powers to those of the Scottish and Welsh Development Agencies in relation to small firms. Thresholds for government support schemes which small firms are unable to cross, the Report said, should be reviewed.

This would be a useful start, but if the long drift towards concentration is to be reversed, much more is needed. The new agency should positively go out and look for products and services which small firms can produce, as COSIRA (Council for Siting Industry in Rural Areas) has done so successfully in rural areas. New firms should be able to qualify for capital loans at a subsidized interest rate, and they should be entitled to similar help when they reach the breakthrough point of rapid growth. This is the stage at which many small innovatory firms go under, because they cannot finance expansion on the scale needed to meet demand. Good legal and accounting services should be readily available through the new agency, which should also offer advice on government schemes that may be helpful. Red tape and form-filling needs to be kept to a minimum, since small firms rarely have the bureaucracy to cope with complicated application forms. The Microelectronic Applications Project introduced by the Labour government of 1976–9 has been successful in attracting several thousand requests for its consultancy scheme, not just because the government met the first £2,000 of the consultant's fees, but because the procedure for applying is so simple.

FINANCE

The loan guarantee proposal should make it easier for the banks to lend money to small firms. But undoubtedly the banking system could be much more helpful than it is. In successful economies like those of Germany and Japan, the banks are much closer to industry than they are in Britain. German banks are often represented on the boards of industrial companies, and there is frequent communication between them. British banks much more often adopt a 'hands-off' stance, though they are willing to offer advice if requested. Too often, the banks only become involved when a rescue operation is under way, as happened with Nation Life and London and County Securities. The Bank of Japan is far more interventionist than the Bank of England, and much closer to government. It is selective both in the credits it advances and in the discount rates it offers, using both weapons to favour industry, and in particular export industry and innovatory firms. The Bank of Japan also consults regularly with the commercial banks, and warns them if it believes advances should be restrained or loans restricted. Japanese banks have favoured forward-looking and efficient firms as compared to failing ones. They have also favoured industry in general as compared to consumer credit, including the credit card system.[24] In Britain, venture capital for small or medium-sized companies is very hard to raise. It is high time British banks launched subsidies to provide venture capital as banks in other countries do.

The Bank of England was nationalized as long ago as 1948, which only goes to show how little difference nationalization can make. As Andrew Shonfield said in a lecture called 'The Politics of the Mixed Economy in the International System of the 1970s',

> The Socialists were concerned above all with the control of what they called 'the commanding heights' of the economy; and their solution was to nationalize them. In the event, the Socialist governments of the post-war period have been able to 'command' precious little from these eminences which they captured or had captured for them.[25]

The Bank of England is unquestionably a commanding height. It is also true that Socialist governments have been able to 'command' precious little from it. The strange neglect of management by Labour thinkers has a great deal to do with the fact that public ownership has so often made so little difference – for it is a company's organization, not its ownership, that really matters, and the Bank's managers are true heirs to its free-market City traditions. The Bank, and the banks, could do much more to encourage small industrial enterprises, but then they could do much more to encourage industry altogether.

In the public sector, government can bypass the banks, making capital available through its own agencies, like the Development Agencies or the National Enterprise Board. The National Enterprise Board was until recently proving a great success, fast-moving, adventurous and yet wise in its judgements. The NEB's terms of reference should be altered to allow it to be a permanent partner in joint public/private enterprises, and also to finance new competitive enterprises in the public sector. So often the public sector has had to rescue ailing enterprises, like Leyland, Chrysler and Rolls-Royce, which remain in the public sector if they continue to make losses and are returned to the private sector if they make a profit. This distinction has been sharpened into a doctrine by Mrs Thatcher's government. It is profoundly demoralizing to the public · sector, and deliberately drives it into being loss-making. It has an interesting parallel with the assisted-places scheme in education; the public sector's successes are to be transferred to the private sector; the failures are to stay where they are. It is no way to administer a mixed economy.

The public sector has not attracted much creative thinking. Socialists tend to argue about the frontiers between the private and public sector, while neglecting what the public sector could become: an example of good practice in consultation and industrial democracy and an area of innovation in both technology and organization. The Post Office was the first industry to have worker representatives on the Board, though consultation in the Post Office had a long and honourable history. The National Coal Board has a structure of consultation stretching from each individual pit to the centre, though joint control was rejected by the National Union of Mineworkers when coal was first nationalized. But most other nationalized industries have not advanced very far.

Nor has there been much organizational innovation in other ways, for example in profit-sharing schemes for workpeople, or in backing industrial cooperatives. The Cooperative Development Agency is just beginning to get some new cooperatives going, however, and there are interesting grassroots stirrings. Among the most exciting developments have been local enterprise trusts and community enterprises. Local enterprise trusts have been set up in some instances by private companies in partnership with local authorities, as in the case of St Helens, where the Pilkington Glass Company was one of the moving forces. In other cases, community enterprises have been financed by public corporations, as with British Steel, which set up Clyde Workshops to house small enterprises able to create permanent jobs for redundant steelworkers, incidentally at a fraction of the cost of job creation by government agencies. Other examples abound: groups of young people doing maintenance and repair work for private residents, assisted in some cases by local authorities; others engaged in offering arts and sports, and ploughing back all the profits they make after drawing their own living expenses; the seconding of executives by big companies to help set up small companies to provide jobs; the industrial cooperatives established in remote communities by the Highlands and Islands Board; and recent schemes for redeveloping derelict inner city areas by linking workshops, service companies and crafts in with residential development – in effect re-creating the organic city of Renaissance Italy.

These developments have the enthusiastic support of many of Britain's best companies, private and public alike. There are firms that are hiving off their new products to autonomous teams to develop, and others that set a limit to the size of any individual plant. Gradually industry is recovering flexibility – or anyway the best of it is. But government policies are crucial to sustaining these new developments; and government policies of both parties have tended to reinforce the momentum towards concentration, creating a dialogue of a limited and sterile kind between the proponents of private concentration and those of public concentration. Yet it is doubtful if people want to work in centralized, concentrated structures, and it is questionable whether these are the most efficient producers of wealth. There has been a growing hostility towards centralization and bureaucracy. Politicians should look at their policy proposals in terms of what people want, how the quality of people's lives can be enriched and made more satisfactory. Reversing the tide of concentration is the first necessary step towards a more decentralized, responsive society; it may also be a crucial step towards controlling the powerful forces of inflation.

9

More Participation: Trade Unions

The industrialized economy, especially one as centralized and concentrated as that of Britain, is heavily dependent on certain essential national services: for instance electricity supply, water, rail and road transport, the docks. The area of dependency has widened to include waste disposal, hospital and ambulance services, and, as the economy modernizes, central computing and data banks as well. If any of these services ceases to operate, the whole economy is imperilled. There are, of course, a whole range of other services and manufacturing industries such as steel or metal manufacturers where stoppages can cripple the economy in time, but the effects are less immediate and imports may provide alternative sources of supply.

It is this interdependence of the economy that makes the power of trade unions such a central issue. Single trade unions have the ability to cut off many countries' economic blood supply. Britain is especially exposed, partly because the labour force is highly organized. About 55 per cent of the British workforce is unionized, compared to under a quarter in the United States. For historical reasons, Britain's unions have tended to develop along craft and occupational lines, rather than on an industry-by-industry basis, which makes incomes policy, industrial democracy and the reform of collective bargaining procedures difficult to achieve. There has been a lot of discussion about merging unions, and some mergers have occurred, but any major restructuring, such as happened in occupied West Germany after the Second World War, is not likely at the present time. Nevertheless, there are considerable strains and tensions in the trade union movement, some of them arising from this outdated and creaky structure. Some unions have suffered heavy losses of membership because of industrial changes; the miners' union and the railwaymen's unions are obvious examples. Others are caught up in disputes about who should represent workers in new trades. Craft unions are separate from general unions, which means that differentials are often a source of ill-feeling between unions. In traditional crafts threatened by advancing technologies, unions can fight for their members' disappearing jobs to the point where the jobs of other unions' members are threatened or destroyed. The printing of newspapers both in the United States and Britain has been frequently disrupted by the efforts of the printers to hold on to their traditional highly paid jobs.

Trade unions have problems of internal communication just as managers in companies do, problems which multiply in very large unions or in those which combine workers in disparate industries within a single general union. Some trade union officials have to be re-elected regularly; others are elected or even appointed for life. Trade union officials have to live with the shop-steward structure in many unions, shop stewards being elected by their fellow-workers to represent them at plant or works level. The dual structure of bargaining in Britain in effect creates two levels of leadership, not one, and there are often stresses between them. National bargains are normally reached between the national officials of a trade union and the representatives of the federation of employers, or, in the case of a national monopoly, the single employer. Where many firms are involved, the national settlement is followed by local negotiations using it as the starting point. Local officials and shop stewards become involved both in local bargaining and in subsequently monitoring the local settlement. So there are two potential lines of influence, one through the full-time officials of national trade unions, the other through shop stewards. It is not unusual for shop stewards and trade union officials to pull different ways and to offer conflicting advice. The involvement of many British trade unions in politics, through their affiliation to the Labour party, can also present problems of communication and indeed of accountability. There are some affiliated unions in which a substantial part of the membership may not be Labour supporters at all.

Trade unions are held responsible for many of Britain's economic weaknesses, but criticism of unions is by no means restricted to Britain.

The power of unions and their irresponsibility, so one would have to conclude from the pronouncements of neoclassical economists, business representatives and conservative parties, is the one single factor (apart, perhaps, from the greed of the OPEC countries) which explains most of what is presently wrong with western economies. By raising the price of unskilled labour beyond its market value, union wages are said to be the major cause of unemployment, and by exploiting the scarcity value of skilled labour, they are said to be directly responsible for wage-push inflation.

Thus writes Fritz Scharpf, Director of the Wissenschaftszentrum, Berlin, in a paper entitled *Capitalism of Yesteryear – and of Tomorrow?*‡[1]

Apart from their effect on wages, trade unions are alleged to disrupt production schedules and delivery dates by strikes, both official and unofficial. The growth and prosperity of industry are damaged by restrictive practices such as overmanning, fragmentation of jobs by craft unions, limits on the output of individual workers or of equipment, and burdensome conditions before agreement can be reached on installing new machinery or introducing new processes. 'Productivity is now importantly hampered by overmanning and restrictive practices which, if they could be reduced or removed, would allow rapid increases in productivity,' concludes the OECD's 1980 Economic Survey of the United Kingdom.

But restrictive practices are by no means limited to the labour market, as the last chapter demonstrates. Much more than the United States, Western Europe has relied on cartels, pricing agreements, market-sharing arrangements and monopolies to limit and restrict competition. What has been true of labour has also been true of business. The strength of organized labour grew relative to that of business in the decades of full employment after the war, so that some trade unions were able to insist upon conditions for recruitment and particular qualifications for skill. In Britain, the folk memory of mass unemployment between the wars has been very slow to fade, perhaps because of the persistence of the class system, perhaps because of relatively low geographic mobility. Restrictive practices have often been adopted as a means of protecting jobs, which in the short run they may do. In some firms the workload during normal working hours has been limited so that workpeople have been able to work long hours of overtime as well. Overtime has become endemic in some industries and is quite often guaranteed.

WAGES AND INFLATION

But trade unions' resistance to wage cuts during recessions, far from damaging industrial economies, has been an important stabilizing factor. Wages and salaries constitute a very large part, usually about three fifths, of the national income. They are therefore the main element in domestic demand. Wage cuts, complemented by cuts in unemployment pay (the 'dole'), helped to precipitate the slump of the 1920s and 1930s. To quote Fritz Scharpf again:

> Perhaps the most important [of the stabilizing factors] is the 'downward stickiness' of wages which are determined by collective bargaining. They have stabilized the income, and thus the demand, of the great majority of wage earners even in recession periods, and they have so far helped to avoid the vicious cycle of downward spiralling demand that caused the great depression.[2]

The trade unions' ability to maintain and increase wages is not, however, equally great in all countries. British trade unions have in recent years succeeded in gaining higher percentage increases in money wages than American and German trade unions; but prices have risen more rapidly too, and real wages in Britain have increased only slowly. American unions are relatively weak outside the traditional industrial regions of the north-east and middle west. The German unions, like the Japanese, work closely with both employers and the government to keep inflation down, seeking improvements in real rather than money wages.

As unemployment rises in the first half of the 1980s, British unions are moderating their claims. The 1980 Treasury forecast for Britain shows average earnings and retail prices moving very closely together until 1983, with earnings falling slightly behind prices in 1981 and moving slightly ahead in 1982. The increase in productivity is also expected to be small, about 1 per cent per annum through the period. The more moderate wage settlements expected, however, will not improve the market for labour; for consumer expenditure is likely to stagnate, while public expenditure and capital investment actually decline. A stagnating economy with rising unemployment is not a propitious atmosphere for rooting out restrictive practices and for improving the productivity on which real increases in earnings are based.

Have the unions been responsible for wage-push inflation? Clearly they bear some responsibility, because they have used their power to push up wages without corresponding productivity gains, and that is bound to be inflationary. Some unions, as already indicated, have deliberately acted to restrict productivity growth, though others deserve more credit than they have got for negotiating agreements to reduce overmanning, or to run down staff as demand declines. Unions certainly influence the rate of inflation. As John Kenneth Galbraith has said, there has been a transfer of power over prices and incomes to the great corporate bodies, including the unions. This conclusion was expressed dramatically by Peter Parker, chairman of British Rail, in a Fabian lecture in February 1979: 'We have long failed to recognize that we are living in a corporate society, that there has been an irreversible shift of power to highly organized functional groups, that it is this that dislocates the workings of our social democracy.'[3]

What is the nature of trade union power? Incomes policies have been most successful where labour is highly organized, and where individual trade unions look to the central union organization or to one major union for guidance. Thus incomes policies worked for many years in Sweden, where the trade unions are cohesively organized within the LO, the trade union federation, and in Holland, where the trade unions were consulted alongside the employers in a council of labour. What is in practice an incomes norm is established in West Germany by the annual negotiation between IG Metall, the metal workers' union, and the major metal manufacturers. This figure, which is influenced by discussions between the government, the DGB (the German trade union federation) and the employers, then acts as a norm for the other bargains, though there may be differences among them in other respects. The German unions are small enough in number and large enough in membership to be able to afford expert staffs, so that they can hold their own in discussions on the economy and on labour's share in national income. The unions then have to win the adherence of their members to the settlements proposed. The simple vertical structure of industrial unions makes this easier in the Federal Republic than it is in Britain. Internecine tensions are minimized, since most grades of worker belong to the same union. Inter-union battles for recognition or over demarcation are rare, and no union can hope to gain members from another by demonstrating militancy or by pursuing disproportionate claims. The job of German trade unions is also eased by the amount of information on the state of the economy and of each individual company available to their members through the system of works councils. German workers know the effect that inflationary settlements will have on employment prospects and on prices because the facts are available to them. They also know when they are getting paid too little. This basis of consultation underpins West Germany's bargaining system. In Britain, a heavy price is paid in suspicion and antagonism because so little information is revealed and so few companies consult their workers.

INCOMES POLICY

Trade unions in Britain have frequently demonstrated their own understanding of the need for incomes policies, and trade union leaders, not least successive General Secretaries of the TUC, have used their influence to construct them. Incomes policies have broken down mainly because trade union members in some crafts or occupations revolted against them, or, more frequently, because their shop stewards did. Writing at the peak of the winter of discontent on 26 January 1979, Peter Jenkins commented: 'If the country threatens to become ungovernable, it is not because of the power of the unions; it is rather because of their powerlessness to govern their own members.'[4]

When a national incomes policy obtains, the national bargain becomes the key one. Indeed, crude incomes policies like those of 1975–7 allow for no additional local bargaining on incomes at all. So shop stewards cannot perform their normal function. It is thus not surprising that shop stewards are often much more hostile towards incomes policies than national officials, elected national leaders or rank-and-file trade unionists. Indeed, throughout the whole three and a half years of the last Labour government's pay policies, public opinion polls registered convincing majority support for them, including majority support from trade union members. But majority support, in the absence of support from either trade union executive committees or shop stewards, did not suffice.

Highly organized corporate groups have moderated recession. They have also exacerbated inflation. It is the job of government to represent the public interest, and not the interest of any particular group where that group's interests conflict with the public interest. That is why it is of the essence of any government accountable to the people that it should not identify too closely with a particular class, profession, occupation or interest. Given the nature of political parties, they will of course lean towards particular groups or classes, and their policies will reflect that. But governments will often have to make decisions between the interests of groups towards which they are well disposed, and the interests of the citizens as a whole. Obviously there can be arguments about the public interest. One party will argue that low taxes and low public expenditure are in the public interest, the other the reverse. Often, however, it is clear where the public interest lies; the pain is not then in choosing the public interest, but in disappointing one's friends and allies.

If the administered prices, wages and salaries that characterize modern mixed economies are engines for inflation, and if it is also true that inflation is not in the public interest, then governments have three choices open to them. The first is to control those bodies that administer prices and pay directly; the second is to try to weaken or destroy them; and the third is to try to persuade them to cooperate in fighting inflation. Let me take each in turn.

Governments can control firms and trade unions directly by incorporating them within the state itself and controlling them by directives or through the party in a one-party state. This has been the pattern adopted in the Soviet bloc, with the state apparatus itself effectively administering prices and incomes. It is a system that has come under increasing strain. Relief from that strain has been found in the black market, in which prices find their own level, in moonlighting and casual work for cash down, and more recently in some publicly permitted private trading around the edges of the state-controlled economy. Private gardens and smallholdings which are allowed to sell their surplus food in the market have flourished in much of Eastern Europe. In Poland, agriculture is largely in the private sector. In Hungary, some small shops and workshops are in the private sector. Nevertheless, the strains are evident, in the queues for scarce consumer goods and sometimes their total disappearance from the shops, and more recently in the massive strikes in Poland demanding the establishment of trade unions independent of the state. Demands for independent trade union bargaining over wages and conditions and independent representation on workers' councils seem likely to spread to other Eastern European countries.

Some governments in the West, in particular Britain and France, have from time to time imposed statutory prices or incomes policies or both on firms and trade unions, relying on the constitutional powers of the executive and the legislature. Usually adopted to meet severe economic crises, statutory prices and incomes policies are too rigid to last for long. Typically they are modified by permitting qualifications or exceptions, such as price increases where imported materials are needed and costs have risen, or wage increases based on higher productivity. The qualifications then arouse feelings of injustice as between one firm or one group of workers and another, and the policies become discredited.

Second, the institutions that establish prices or wages can be weakened or destroyed. Conservative parties believe that high unemployment will weaken the trade unions, and lessen their bargaining power. Socialist governments may have recourse to investigating prices or freezing them in order to weaken the power of big business, though they seem reluctant to attack the cartels and oligopolies that in fact administer prices. There are grounds for countering the power of the great corporate interests, not least by encouraging a more decentralized economy. But unemployment is a desperate remedy, tantamount to shooting a patient with a high fever as a way of curing the fever.

THE SOCIAL CONTRACT

The third approach is that of seeking the cooperation of the corporate powers. Indeed, the very words change, so that the corporate powers become social partners in a social contract, or leading instruments in *konzertierte Aktion*, the melodious German name for the process. Voluntary incomes policies and voluntary price restraint are the objectives of this third way.

Obviously, any such voluntary policy has to be flexible over time, responding to the state of the economy nationally and internationally. Therefore machinery for consultation has to exist, in which business and trade union leaders as well as government are represented. In Britain the one forum in which the 'social partners' and the government already meet, the National Economic Development Council, might be adapted for the purpose of working out an incomes and prices norm in the light of the economic prospects for the country, so long as its other functions were not jeopardized. Other countries have economic and social councils of which the social partners are members, and this is another possible pattern.

Agreement between the leaders of the trade unions, business and government is a necessary step, but it is far from sufficient. In any pluralist society, the leaders will have to win the agreement of their followers, and this is the central issue. Presentation of the facts and a major public educational campaign by the social partners will help. But ultimately the process of consultation cannot be limited to a few at the top. It has to be carried right down to the local plant, office and workshop. The repeated collapse of incomes and prices policy in Britain, after brave and even for a time successful attempts, spells out the impossibility of imposing a lead from the top in such sensitive matters.

At this stage, a brief account of the experience of the 1974–9

Labour government's incomes policy may help us to avoid making the same mistakes. It took eighteen months for the 1974 Labour government to realize that the combination of threshold payments (the legacy of the previous Conservative government) and free collective bargaining was taking the economy to the brink of disaster. Annual inflation rates, already rising fast when the government took office in March 1974, reached the high twenties by the spring of 1975. Wages and prices pursued one another in a race that could have no winners. By May 1975 the government and the unions alike realized that the economic situation could not be allowed to deteriorate further. In a series of informal meetings between a small group of Cabinet Ministers and the leaders of the most powerful trade unions, the so-called Neddy six (being the representatives of the unions on the National Economic Development Council), a crude voluntary incomes policy was stitched together. It was put together against the background of a 'social contract' in which the Labour government committed itself to a programme of legislation and social policies of particular interest to the trade unions. Its central element had been proposed in a speech by Jack Jones, then General Secretary of the biggest British trade union, the Transport and General Workers' Union. It was for a £6 a week flat rate increase for everyone, regardless of their existing wage or salary level, with a ceiling of £8,500 a year beyond which no rise at all would be paid. The government tried to make the £6 a week into a maximum, but most settlements were for £6. The sheer simplicity of the idea captured the public imagination, and made the policing of settlements, by the unions and by public opinion, remarkably easy. In its first year the policy was overwhelmingly adhered to.

The second year, which ran from August 1976 to July 1977, was even more successful, and was certainly tougher. The craft unions and the powerful engineering union were worried at the erosion of skill and other differentials implicit in a flat-rate incomes policy, so they sought to modify it in the second year. A rather more complicated formula was devised, providing for a minimum increase of £2.50 a week to protect the low-paid, and a maximum of £4.00 a week for the better-paid, the overall percentage rate being just under 5 per cent. Again, the policy was adhered to almost everywhere, and inflation rates began to fall rapidly, even though the declining value of the pound worked in the opposite direction. But resistance began to grow, especially among skilled workers and the better-paid. The third year of incomes policy no longer commanded the support of the Trades Union Congress, though the TUC and the individual unions did not actively resist it. A norm of 10 per cent, the flat-rate element having been abandoned, was largely followed, though some settlements were massaged a little to bring them within the norm – for instance by allowing something extra for fringe benefits, more time off or better pensions.

This third year of reasonable success, even without TUC backing, may have made the government over-confident. It announced a 5 per cent norm for 1978/9, which on all the statistical projections available to the government would have brought about the biggest real increase in the standard of living of wage-earners of any figure chosen. A higher norm was accepted for those earning less than £44.50 a week. But prices were still increasing at 8 per cent per annum in July 1978. True, they were expected to fall to below the 5 per cent norm by 1979, and the norm itself would probably have represented 7 per cent or 8 per cent on earnings with overtime and other factors taken into account. But an incomes target below price rises looked like an attempt to cut living standards. Nor did the government mount a public campaign to get its case across, as it had in 1976 when a letter went to every household in the country explaining the objective of the incomes policy. The unions, for their part, moved from neutrality to hostility. Their leaders finally refused to discuss incomes policy at all, though the balance of opinion among them was tantalizingly close; the General Council of the TUC only rejected a proposal to take part in discussions on a fourth year of incomes policy by the casting vote of the chairman.

So near and yet so far. By the autumn of 1978, union after union was refusing to settle for 5 per cent. A last-ditch attempt in the Cabinet to establish a new norm of 8 per cent, in line with inflation, failed to carry the day, though, with hindsight, it seems that an 8 per cent norm might have won trade union support. Lorry drivers went on strike in November 1978 and were soon followed by workers in local government and the health services, disrupting schools, hospitals, rubbish collection and even, in some areas, the burial of the dead. The 'winter of discontent', as it came to be called, effectively destroyed the government, in spite of a remarkable narrowing of the gap between the major parties during the election campaign of April and May 1979. For the third time since the war, the attempt to enforce an incomes policy had been a decisive factor, perhaps *the* decisive factor, in bringing a government down.

Given the structure of British trade unionism, with its vigorous shop-steward movement, it is necessary that any incomes policy should leave some room for local bargaining. Bargaining need not be only about wages, though there might be some room for variations around the national norm. Indeed, it might be a very good thing for the trade union movement to widen its bargaining aims to include the training of young people, the retraining of older workers, machinery for information and consultation and the unification of working conditions, as a few unions already do. Distinctions between who eats in which canteen, who clocks on and who doesn't, who needs permission to leave the job for an hour and who doesn't, who gets a company car and who doesn't are much more pervasive in Britain than in the enterprises of her main competitors in Europe or the United States. In West Germany, works councils have set the improvement of conditions of work as a major objective, and with considerable success. Trade unions in Britain would get more public support, and new members too, if they widened their objectives in this way. And some of these objectives would be most effectively pursued through local bargaining.

INDUSTRIAL DEMOCRACY

The response of rank-and-file union members to incomes policy will depend on whether they accept the need for it, and whether they think it is fair. The involvement of workpeople in the decisions firms make, through consultation and through participation in works committees or at boardroom level, provides a much stronger foundation for voluntary incomes and prices policies than the sporadic communication and confrontation that exist in many British firms. Obviously there are real conflicts of interest on the distribution of a firm's earnings as between higher profits and higher wages. Differentials between workpeople and between them and line managers or senior managers can be another source of disagreement. But the genuine conflicts are often overlaid by conflicts based on mutual ignorance, or on a failure to understand that firms need to invest in future products and sell current products in what may be competitive markets. Industrial democracy, like training in basic economics, produces a better informed workforce and a better informed management. It is simply true that voluntary incomes and prices policies have worked best in those countries where industrial democracy is most strongly established.

Industrial democracy is not only relevant to the success or failure of incomes and prices policies. It is also highly relevant to the introduction of the new technologies and to whether their advent will be resisted. In Chapter 8, I pointed out that the firms interviewed for the Policy Studies Institute project on the application of microelectronics to manufacturing industry reported no obstruction from trade unions to its introduction (though in some cases the workforce had not been told about the firm's intentions). Trade unions in Britain, as in Germany, France and North America, have in fact done a great deal of work on the impact of microelectronics on their members' prospects. Several unions in Britain, and the Trades Union Congress itself, have produced detailed and impressive reports. The European Trades Union Institute, the Nordic Trades Union Council, the DGB (Deutsche Gewerkschaftbund) and the American trade union federation, AFL-CIO, have all given their member unions detailed guidance. The guidance proposes that unions should not oppose the introduction of new technologies which could benefit the living standards of their members. But unions should insist on being involved in the changes that are coming, in protecting those whose jobs will be affected or more radically in protecting existing employment levels and in safeguarding workers against being downgraded to lower wage-levels or to dull and routine jobs.

Some unions have already been involved in negotiating new technology agreements in a wide range of industries, particularly engineering, telecommunications and office work.[5] All the agreements have clauses stressing the importance of consultation and discussion on the introduction of new technologies. Some specify the information to be made available and at what stage. Many establish joint machinery where it does not already exist; in some cases, consultation on the new technologies will be conducted in a separate committee or in a sub-committee of the existing joint consultative committee. A number of unions have managed to negotiate 'status quo' clauses, i.e. that there will be no change in the status quo without the agreement of both management and unions. Agreement that there should be no compulsory redundancies is also usual, though few unions have won a guarantee of no reduction in existing employment levels. Some new technology agreements also deal with employee training including union participation in training syllabuses, training for union representatives on joint technology committees, the design of equipment and the special physical and mental stresses involved in long periods of using visual display units.

Through the need for participation in the introduction of new technologies, management and unions are having to establish consultative machinery where none exists, and to reconstruct it where it does. Those firms who want to move ahead quickly will achieve trade union cooperation if they offer participation in exchange; otherwise they will face resistance and obstruction. The new technologies offer an opportunity to widen industrial democracy at the plant and office level, where it matters most. Whether joint consultation at that level leads on to participation in the boardroom is a matter that can be left to each company and its unions to decide.

More difficult is the question of how the workforce in each firm should be represented. In the Cabinet committee which drew up the 1979 White Paper on industrial democracy, there were differing views on whether workers should elect their representatives to plant and company committees or whether they should be nominated by the trade unions (the 'single channel'). The issue is far from simple. In Sweden and the Federal Republic of Germany most firms have only one trade union, so there is no need to secure agreement among them before candidates for election can be put forward. In Britain, as many as twenty unions may represent the employees of large firms, and four or five unions in a firm are commonplace. In these circumstances, a straightforward election would be likely to lead to all the representatives coming from the biggest unions, the rest being unrepresented.

But the nomination of a single list by agreement between the unions in a plant or firm offends the principle of democratic choice. The workers may object to one or more of the people selected to represent them, yet they would have no power to reject him or her other than by rejecting the whole slate and jeopardizing participation itself. One way out of this dilemma would be for the unions in a multi-union plant to agree on constituencies representing each union on a weighted basis, with an election based on a secret ballot between candidates who were members of the appropriate union, some of whom might carry official endorsement.

Industrial democracy has not attracted consistent support from most trade unions, and the trade unions themselves are profoundly divided on the form it should take, many preferring a consultative structure to one of statutory participation on the lines proposed in the Bullock Report. If the unions are divided, however, much of management feels threatened by the idea of industrial democracy. So for years there has been a stalemate on the subject, and governments intervene at their peril. Yet, if only because there has to be effective consultation on technological change, the position cannot be left where it is. Indeed, in my view industrial democracy could usher in much better relations in industry, greater cooperation in improving the productivity of all factors of production and a better understanding of the need for voluntary incomes and prices policies to combat inflation. Many of Britain's economic problems are rooted in institutional rigidities or, as in this case, institutional conservatism. This one reform could bring in its wake a long-delayed rejuvenation. We should not be daunted by the difficulties, but rather invigorated by the possibilities.

10

Social Services: Involving People

There are many contenders for public expenditure, for instance law and order, defence, education and training, health and the social services. Conservative governments are inclined to support increases in public expenditure on law and order and defence, and to want to make savings on social expenditure. It is not easy to do so. Some of the claims for increasing social expenditure are consequences of the growing numbers entitled to pensions and benefits, sometimes called transfer payments. Rising unemployment exacts a heavy public cost in unemployment benefit, redundancy payments, supplementary benefit, and in such means-tested benefits as free school meals for children and rent rebates to which most unemployed families are entitled. The proportion of retired people is also growing, mainly because people are living longer; indeed the number of people over seventy-five, and the proportion of the population that they represent, is growing faster than any other section of the population, including the sixty-fives to seventy-fives. It is the very old who make most demands on the personal social services and on the health services, because of their dependency and their often indifferent state of health. Housing, another significant contender, cannot make such a strong claim to larger resources on demographic grounds. Nevertheless, the high birth rates of 1957 to 1965 are beginning to turn into high family formation rates, and many young people are unable to afford to buy a house.

The contenders are no longer battling for a growing social budget, they are fighting over a shrinking one. The reaction against 'big government', high public expenditure and high taxes in the

Western industrial countries has reversed the earlier trend for public expenditure to take a rising share of the gross domestic product. The 1979 election in Britain and the 1980 federal elections in West Germany and the United States were not fought on promises of expanding social services and more generous welfare provision. They were fought between parties advocating substantial reductions in public expenditure, lower taxes and conservative budgeting, and parties arguing for the status quo or, at most, modest improvements in one area balanced by savings in another.

Admittedly the tax-cutters and welfare critics lost their sharp edge once the consequences of chopping back on social services became clear, as already mentioned with regard to California's Proposition 13. In Britain, local authorities which increased their rates (local property taxes) to offset the cut in central government support for local government services, like education and housing, did not lose voters' support in the local government elections of May 1980. But there may be a threshold beyond which it is difficult to push public expenditure, though that threshold is likely to differ from country to country and according to whether national income is growing or not. It also differs according to the pattern of taxation. There is reason to believe that taxpayers are more aware of the burden of direct taxation than of indirect taxation. Where consumers enjoy a steady improvement year by year in their private standard of living, they seem better disposed to contributing more to the social services. A study on the perception of poverty in Europe[1] showed less support for egalitarian policies and a much greater readiness to blame the poor for their poverty in slowly growing Britain than in fast-growing France, the Netherlands or West Germany. In the United States, where growth has been slow, the poor are also popular scapegoats.

Growth rates are in no way correlated with the proportion of the gross domestic product going to public expenditure, whatever the monetarists may say. Public expenditure as a percentage of gross domestic product averaged 43.7 per cent in the Western European countries between 1976 and 1978, the Netherlands and Sweden being at the very top with over 55 per cent, and Spain at the bottom with 25.2 per cent. The United States and Japan were both much lower than the West European average, at 34·2 per cent and 28·6 per cent respectively, for reasons I shall come back to.

Table 2. Public Expenditure as a Percentage of GDP 1976–8
(three-year average)

Australia	35·2
Austria	45·8
Belgium	48·2
Canada	40·3
Denmark	(47·6)
Finland	40·1
France	44·4
Germany (FRG)	44·7
Greece	–
Ireland*	46·3
Italy	43·0
Japan	28.6
Netherlands	55·3
New Zealand	36·3
Norway	50.6
Portugal*	34·1
Spain*	25·2
Sweden	58·5
Switzerland	–
United Kingdom	44·2
United States	34·2
OECD average (non-weighted)†	43·7

* Latest year available, Ireland and Spain 1977, Portugal 1976.
† Excludes Greece, Ireland, Portugal, Spain and Switzerland.
Source: National Accounts of OECD Countries, Paris, OECD, 1980.

Transfer payments, mainly social security benefits of various kinds, amounted to about a fifth of most countries' gross domestic product, but were much higher in the Netherlands, which increased benefits substantially at the time of its natural gas boom. They were much lower in the United States and Japan. Final consumption, other than defence – that is to say, expenditure on schools, hospitals, community services and so on – averaged about 14½ per cent for the

Table 3. Public Expenditure by (i) *Final Consumption,* (ii) *Transfers and Subsidies,* (iii) *Interest on Public Debt and* (iv) *Investments as a Percentage of GDP 1976–8*

	Final Consumption	Subsidies and Transfers	Interest on Public Debt	Investment
Australia	16.1	9.7	2.4	–
Austria	17.6	20.1	1.8	5.4
Belgium	17.8	22.0	4.6	3.1
Canada	20.3	12.1	4.4	3.2
Denmark	(25.0)	(16.1)	(1.0)	(4.4)
Finland	19.8	14.1	0.7	4.4
France	14.9	23.8	1.3	3.3
Germany (FRG)	20.1	18.1	1.7	3.3
Greece	15.7	11.4	1.6	–
Ireland*	18.6	18.6	4.9	4.1
Italy	15.3	18.4	5.1	3.6
Japan	9.7	10.4	1.9	5.6
Netherlands	18.2	29.0	3.0	3.5
New Zealand	18.1	14.5	2.5	5.2
Norway	18.1	24.1	2.9	4.9
Portugal*	14.2	15.4	1.1	3.1
Spain*	9.7	11.2	0.5	2.5
Sweden	27.7	22.8	2.6	4.4
Switzerland	13.0	12.2	2.1	–
United Kingdom	20.9	14.3	4.5	3.5
United States	18.4	11.3	2.7	1.7
OECD average (non-weighted)†	18.4	17.5	2.7	4.1

* Latest year available Ireland and Spain 1977; Portugal 1976.

† OECD average excludes Greece, Ireland, Portugal, Spain and Switzerland because certain series could not be reconstructed for those countries up to 1955.

Source: National Accounts of OECD Countries, Paris, OECD, 1980.

OECD as a whole. Only Sweden and Denmark were far above the average, Japan and Spain far below.

It is certain that public expenditure as a proportion of the gross domestic product of Western European countries has declined in the last two or three years, and will decline further. Britain may be taken as a not untypical case. As Table 4 shows, total public expenditure was 44.5 per cent of gross domestic product, taking the three years between 1974 and 1976 together. This average masks a big leap between 1973/4 and 1974/5, from 40.5 per cent to 46 per cent, a percentage sustained in 1975/6. The Government White Paper, Command 7439, then charts the rapid decline from 1975/6 to 1977/8, followed by a modest recovery in 1978/9.

Table 4. *The Changing Pattern of Public Spending in the British Economy* (*as a percentage of gross domestic product*)

	1973/4	1974/5	1975/6	1976/7	1977/8	1978/9
Total public spending	$40\frac{1}{2}$	46	$46\frac{1}{2}$	44	$40\frac{1}{2}$	42

Source: Cmnd 7439, January 1979.

Following the general election and the change of government in May 1979, the Conservative government announced its intention to cut public expenditure in real terms by 5 per cent, and to reduce it as a proportion of gross domestic product. This goal has proved elusive, mainly because of the massive increase in unemployment. If the 5 per cent were adhered to, public expenditure would fall below 40 per cent.

Public expenditure will have a falling share of a declining economy in Britain, and at best a constant share of a slowly growing economy in West Germany and France. This double constraint coincides with increasing needs. The inescapable conclusion seems to be that the standards of the social services, or access to them, or both, are bound to suffer.

It can be argued that the share of public expenditure should be increased and that different economic policies would lead to higher growth. That may well be so, but given the time and investment needed to reverse economic direction and to achieve higher growth, and given the fall in tax revenues because of the recession, no dramatic increase in public expenditure is likely to be feasible in the

near future. The sources of taxation can certainly be widened, to
include taxation on accumulations of wealth of say £150,000 or
more. There is a case for higher indirect taxes on luxury goods,
though in a recession additional expenditure taxes can throw more
people out of work and bankrupt more companies. The wide range
of allowances and exemptions that can be claimed against tax could
be drastically narrowed; the present system has a pervasive aura of
unfairness. So much depends on whether the taxpayer has a
mortgage and, if so, how large a mortgage; on whether he or she
pays on a pay-as-you-earn basis or is self-employed, and, if he is
self-employed, on the ingenuity of his or her accountant. Yet even if
new taxes were to be introduced, and if public expenditure could
be got back to 44 or 45 per cent of gross domestic product or
even more, the finance for major improvements in the social services
is not going to be available this side of much higher growth rates
in the British economy. The same holds for other Western
economies as well.

PRIVATIZATION

Conservatives have an answer: to hand over parts of the social
services to the private sector. It is private provision of medical
services that largely explains the much lower proportion of public
expenditure I have noted in the United States, even though health
takes a larger share of the gross national product in the USA than it
does in Britain. Japan has a system of company-financed welfare,
which enables the government's share in social expenditure to be
much less than in Western Europe. Redundancies, for instance,
rarely happen in Japan; people remain with their companies,
shunted into quiet by-ways and often under-employed, but they are
not dismissed and left for the state social security system to support.
Pension provision is largely dependent on company pension
schemes.

Privatization does not therefore necessarily mean a lower
standard of provision for the individual. Those employed by a
strong and stable company will benefit from good pensions. Those
in weak firms or badly paid occupations will suffer, and their
employers may be unable to bear the costs. Similarly the variation

in private medical provision is well known. The young and healthy can get private medical insurance for reasonable premiums. But for those who were old or ill it became so expensive in the United States to take out private medical insurance that the US Federal Government had to introduce Medicare and Medicaid for the elderly and the very poor. In Western Europe, privatization more often means inducing the individual to make provision for himself over and above what the state provides. Alternatively it can mean passing the burden back to industry. Firms may provide pension schemes, private medical insurance schemes and even schemes to help finance private education for the children of their senior employees. Such fringe benefits can be a substantial addition to the normal salary.

Privatization is not the only solution advanced to cut down the burden of public expenditure. The most common one is simply to cut staff and services, and let the consequences fall where they may. The existence of statutory commitments, for instance to contributors to national insurance funds, as well as political commitments, means that capital programmes usually get hit first. The public is immediately aware of higher prescription charges or more expensive school meals. Postponing new hospitals or ceasing to repair schools and houses isn't much noticed until the waiting lists lengthen or the school roof lets in the rain.

Another approach, rather similar to privatization, is for the government to maintain an individual's entitlement to a benefit, but to shift the cost to industry. This has been proposed in Britain for short-term sickness benefit. The shift of responsibility can be complete, as in this proposal, or partial. Firms that provide medical treatment in their plants and firms that provide training reduce the financial burdens that would otherwise have to be borne by the public services. In a period of decline or of slow growth, however, industry is not in a position to carry additional financial responsibilities. Nor would industry willingly accept increases in social security contributions, the major source of revenue along with taxation from which pensions and benefits are financed.*

* The UK government's raising of national insurance contributions announced in November 1980 led to an angry outcry from the Confederation of British Industry.

Increases in contributions push up the non-wage cost of labour and are likely to discourage firms from employing more people.

Does all this mean that there can be no hope of improvements in the public services for years to come, and that we will be lucky to avoid a serious decline in the standard of service offered? Is the welfare state withering away? I have argued in this book that what is needed if the quality of human lives is to be enriched and improved is not just economic growth but also institutional change. Institutional rigidities and corporate interests mean that our existing resources are used much less effectively than they could be. What is true of industry is, despite the great differences in motivation, true of the welfare state as well.

THE 'PROFESSIONALIZATION OF EVERYONE'

The welfare state has become highly institutionalized. It has taken care out of the hands of the family and out of the local community into institutions staffed by professionals. These institutions often have elaborate hierarchies: '. . . the Welfare State institutionalizes a particular way of looking at the delivery of social services . . . it institutionalizes the professional value system . . . To exaggerate only a little, the implicit ideal of Welfare State services is the "professionalization of everyone" working in the social services.' So wrote Rudolf Klein in *Social Policy in the Eighties*, a paper given at the OECD conference on social policy in October 1980.[2] Professional influence on the welfare state is very great. The social services are highly organized by professional associations and by trade unions, and these include some of the toughest negotiators in the business. The medical consultants, for instance, are legendary in government circles for the determination with which they pursue their collective aims. Indeed, the clients' interests sometimes seem secondary to those of the professions. Those who staff the welfare state are naturally defenders of the status quo. They would like more resources, but they are resistant to changing the distribution of the resources they already have. Yet this is the only way improvement can come, given a static or falling social budget.

The welfare state has, again like industry, tended towards

centralization and concentration. In the 1960s, the prevailing fashion for centralization led to the closure of cottage hospitals and other local hospitals in favour of huge district hospitals with highly sophisticated equipment.

It was argued that this expensive equipment could only be used economically if it served a substantial population, since at any one time only a relatively small proportion of people would require intensive care or advanced specialized treatment. The argument was convincing in its way, but the cost of a bed in a district general hospital is much higher than in a cottage hospital. So, given the limits on its resources, the health service found itself unable to provide enough beds, in particular for routine operations like hysterectomies or the replacement of arthritic hip joints. The waiting lists lengthened. Yet some of those in district hospitals could be looked after much less expensively in a local hospital, where they would also be more accessible to their relatives and friends. The medical services, with their emphasis on expensive and sophisticated curative medicine and their relative neglect of preventive medicine, are yet another example of the attraction and influence of high technology.

Building big instead of small seduced the architects and town planners too. The late 1950s and the 1960s have left Western Europe and North America with a legacy of tower blocks and huge municipal estates. The tower blocks were, and are, unsuitable for both the young and the old, yet families were often housed in them. Young children could not play safely many storeys below where their mother or father was working. Cooped up all day in a flat with nothing to see but a landscape of more blocks, young children became either obstreperous or apathetic. For elderly people, tower blocks could be a sentence of solitary confinement. There is no life of the street to enjoy. The lifts are sometimes out of action because of vandalism or mechanical failure, isolating anyone who cannot manage flight after flight of often dirty and foul-smelling stairs. Huge municipal or council estates, even where the houses themselves are low-rise and have gardens, may not be much better. Many were built without any amenities like halls or community rooms, pubs or churches. They are now camps of brick semis, windy and impersonal, offering no visual satisfaction and arousing neither imagination nor curiosity in those who live there. Families and individuals rehoused in such soulless accommodation often preferred the decrepit back-to-backs or shabby Victorian terraces where at least the life of the neighbourhood flowed down the streets and through the back alleys.

As with industry, the problems of communication and understanding grew as the process of concentration and centralization continued. But the social services are more open to public pressure than industry is. People simply refused to live in tower blocks and high-rise estates. Some have become derelict and others have been pulled down. Grassroots campaigners fought against the closure of local hospitals and village schools, often with great energy and passion. By the end of the 1970s, government departments were no longer willing to sanction high-rise residential buildings, massive district hospitals or huge comprehensive schools.

THE COMMUNITY AND THE WELFARE STATE

Can the welfare state be made less bureaucratic and brought closer to the communities from which its clients come, even without much extra money? Yes, it can, and in the course of doing so, the quality of service may actually be improved.

The social services lend themselves to participation, not just by their workers, but by the community as well. Given that professional interests and the public interest in the social services may diverge, it is important that workers and clients are both represented on participatory bodies. Governing bodies of schools should include parents, teachers and, if their age is appropriate, pupils as well. Health authorities, as well as community health councils, should include elected representatives of the local community they serve and of the patients within it – not merely individuals appointed to speak for them – as well as representatives of doctors and health service workers. Tenants should take part in the management of their houses and housing estates.

But participation in the government of schools, hospitals and housing estates is only half the battle. The welfare state is unique in that it also attracts volunteers willing to participate in working for it for nothing as well as in helping to govern it. Unemployment, shorter hours and early retirement are likely to produce more potential volunteers. Many of the 'young elderly' – men and women who are in their sixties and early seventies, active and in good health – welcome the opportunity to help in hospitals and the personal social services. Married women at home or with part-time jobs often take part in the work of local primary schools, listening to children read, or helping them to choose books or to dress and undress. The amount of voluntary work that is done depends above all on the attitude of professional staff, trade unions, matrons, heads, teachers. Its availability is limited by the demand for it and the restrictions placed upon it, rather than by the supply.

A particularly striking example of the readiness of people to volunteer their services was the Adult Literacy Campaign, launched in 1975 by the British Association of Settlements, a voluntary body, in conjunction with the British Broadcasting Corporation. It was estimated by the BAS that there were some two million illiterate or semi-literate adults in Britain. Through a series of broadcasts, the BBC made people familiar with the problem and put illiterate individuals in touch with a voluntary tutor. Suitable textbooks and reading material were also prepared. The response was astonishing. Seventy-five thousand people volunteered to teach an illiterate adult, on the basis of a one-to-one tutorial. Over 100,000 adults became literate in the scheme's first two years. Nothing could have shown more strikingly the size of the reservoir of willing and often qualified people only waiting to be asked to help.

Apart from using volunteers to complement the existing services, there is also tremendous scope for organizing support from the local community. Local radio is being used increasingly to find what help might be available for the needs of particular clients of the welfare services: who wants to foster a child, who can offer short-stay accommodation to an elderly person, who is prepared to befriend an ex-prisoner or a child in a residential home. Groups with a common problem can be brought together by radio and television, again mainly at local or regional level, and can then form mutually supportive self-help organizations. Such organizations have been formed locally and nationally; to mention only a few, among victims of multiple sclerosis, parents of spastic children, and among single parents, where Gingerbread and other organizations have provided systematic support, advice and help. Limited financial help from central or local government towards premises and administrative expenses for mutual support groups can assist them, at minimal cost, to reach many people who are trying to maintain their independence in the community.

Another significant development has been the putting together of artificial family units able to meet some of each other's needs. Mentally handicapped people, or those trying to rehabilitate themselves after long periods in institutional care or in prison, may not survive in the outside world if they live alone with only an occasional visit from a social worker. As members of a 'family' made up of people like themselves, but of different sexes and from different generations, their chances are much better and their lives more satisfying. Furthermore, the social worker can then advise and counsel the 'family' rather than isolated individuals. Lonely individuals can also be introduced into existing families. An imaginative scheme to get families with young children to adopt a pensioner living alone was tried in a poor district of Glasgow with considerable success; Kent County Council runs an 'Adopt a Granny' scheme. Many retired people have time to give and no one to give it to; many children need time and attention but may not get it if their families are large or both parents work. The re-creation of 'family' units may be one of the most successful ways to decentralize the caring services and to make resources go further.

The ready access to information offered by the new technologies can assist the welfare services in other ways, though it will require a change in professional attitudes. The Post Office's viewdata service, Prestel, already carries information prepared by the Consumers' Association on the various benefits available to claimants with different needs. Access to such information through private television sets or through television receivers in public libraries or Citizens' Advice Bureaux will quickly create a much better briefed clientele for welfare services. The idea can be extended widely, to information about local schools and further education courses and leisure activities available to the young or the old. People who are housebound or bedbound can be linked together in conversation circles through microelectronics. There are now effective and inexpensive means of breaking down isolation, relieving loneliness, and using social workers more efficiently than hitherto, especially when making home visits. Indeed, given much cheaper access to two-way communication, many semi-dependent people who would otherwise have become institutionalized will be able to live in the community. The statutory staff of the welfare services could become the core of a more flexible and responsive network in which institutional care is used only intermittently or as a last resort.

Agreement about employment levels in the social services is a prerequisite of such flexibility. It is unreasonable to expect statutory staff to cooperate with volunteers or with the local communities if they are simply making themselves redundant. But it is not beyond the bounds of possibility that such agreements might be reached. There is an obvious parallel with the position of firms embarking upon new technologies, where technological agreements require guarantees for existing employees in exchange for cooperation. Recasting the welfare state into a dual system, one part consisting of established social workers, health workers and teachers, the other of volunteers working with them and under their guidance and supervision, is going to take a lot of determination to achieve, even with some form of employment agreement. Statutory workers are suspicious of volunteers, especially where volunteers may replace them. Professional associations have battled for recognition of qualified status; many volunteers will not be appropriately qualified and hence there is a fear that professional standards will be diluted. It is a familiar enough pattern. But those attracted to work in the social services do so often because they like caring for other people. They have a genuine concern for their well-being. Many will agree to accept voluntary help, as indeed many do already, where it promises a better life for those in need. An attempt to create a more autonomous, community-based and devolved welfare state could elicit a favourable response, providing the professionals did not believe it was merely window-dressing for yet another reduction in the resources available for the social services.

II

Education: Good Schools and Bad Classes

In the intensifying competition for markets with the newly industrializing countries of the Third World, the older industrialized countries are often said to have one great advantage, their education systems. Most have had compulsory primary education for a century; many have had compulsory secondary education for a generation or more. Almost all the citizens of the OECD countries and of the Soviet bloc are literate, most are basically numerate, and a large minority have more advanced professional and technical qualifications.

This educational base gives the older industrial countries a head start in exploiting the new technologies, which require basic understanding of language and mathematics and some knowledge of how to handle and organize information. It is the greatest advantage they have, since their costs of labour are much higher than in the newly industrializing countries. Switzerland and Sweden have shown that countries with few natural advantages can sustain high standards of living by the intelligent deployment of a highly qualified workforce. But the key phrase is 'highly qualified'. The older industrial countries cannot risk a decline in the quality of their education and training. Yet financial resources are under great pressure, and expenditure on education is unlikely to grow at a time when pupil numbers are falling fast.

THE COMPREHENSIVE SCHOOL

Several Western European countries have been passing through a troubled transition from vertically segregated, selective systems of secondary education to comprehensive schools for which entry is unselective. For the lower secondary stage, up to sixteen, the transition has been completed in the Scandinavian countries. Attention is now directed to the upper secondary stage, to breaking down the long-established distinction between academic and vocational education by offering courses in both in the same institution. Britain and France are still in the transitional stage, the progress towards comprehensive education having proved highly controversial in both countries. Nevertheless, in 1979 Britain had over 80 per cent of secondary school children in comprehensive schools. West Germany is at the other end of the spectrum, with only 4 per cent in comprehensive schools apart from West Berlin and Hesse. West Berlin is now largely comprehensive; Hesse has two fifths of its secondary school children in comprehensive schools.

The comprehensive reform, which has engaged so much of the energy of educators and education authorities in the last twenty years, is controversial mainly because it is widely believed that academically able children suffer from being educated together with their less able contemporaries. The debate has centred on systems, not on schools. Would a comprehensive system produce better or worse results academically and socially than a selective system? Or would the results vary according to whether children were average, above average or below average academically? For Western Europe, so dependent on a good educational base, the answers to such questions matter.

Bit by bit, the answers are emerging. The most significant single piece of research undertaken in Britain has been *Progress in Secondary Schools*, based on the work of the National Child Development Study, a longitudinal study of over 16,000 people born in Great Britain between 3 and 9 March 1958.[1] The findings of the study were surprising only to those who were deeply prejudiced against comprehensive schools. 'Those in comprehensive schools did as well and as badly as if selection had still operated and some had gone to grammars and the rest to secondary moderns', the report concludes. Contrary to popular belief, children who were above average at eleven were doing at least as well in comprehensive schools at the age of sixteen as they would have been doing in grammar schools, and considerably better than if they had been in secondary modern schools. The very slow learners also did rather better. The broad range of average children achieved standards that were much the same in all three types of school. The intake into comprehensive schools in 1969, the year when the cohort being studied entered secondary schools, had predominantly manual-worker parents, a slightly higher proportion than in the case of secondary modern schools.

The social case for the comprehensive school has always been unanswerable. By educating children of different backgrounds and of different abilities together, comprehensive schools begin to break down class barriers and the mutual ignorance of different social groups, and create the context for a more democratic, open and unprejudiced society. Even the ancient and costly antagonisms between management and workers in industry, if tackled both through education and through industrial democracy, may begin to disappear. The only conceivable argument against comprehensive education is the educational one, that children's academic achievements will be less good if they are educated together rather than being segregated according to their abilities.

The National Child Development Study does not prove that children do decisively better in comprehensive schools, but it shows convincingly that they do as well as they would in segregated schools. Given that comprehensives were 'creamed'* of their most able potential students in the period studied, the academic results are the more remarkable. Yet creaming of comprehensive schools will continue for two reasons. Local education authorities will not be pressed by a Conservative government to complete the change-over to comprehensive schools. If they decide to retain one or two grammar schools, that will be permitted under the terms of the 1980 Education Act. So the progress of comprehensive education is likely to be stalled or even, in part, reversed.

---

* 'Creaming' describes the process of taking the most able children out of the comprehensive system and sending them to selective schools – either the remaining grammar schools or the independent schools through schemes for giving parents assistance with the fees.

INDEPENDENT SCHOOLS

In Britain, the independent schools continue to take 7–8 per cent of secondary school pupils. While these children, according to the National Child Development Study, did not score on average as high on tests of general ability as children entering grammar or direct-grant schools, they were well ahead of those entering the secondary modern or comprehensive schools. Their social background was markedly different, only 15 per cent of them having parents with manual jobs.

'Creaming' not only affects the chances of far more children than the minority of able youngsters directly involved; it also weakens the support for maintained schools more generally. Many of the most articulate and influential parents have professional and executive jobs, and these are the very parents who most often try to get their children into selective or independent schools. This is not confined only to Britain. The United States school system with its century-old tradition of neighbourhood high schools has suffered grievously in some districts from the flight of educated middle-class parents. The leaders of the community no longer have their children in its schools, as they once did. In Britain, the tradition never existed.

The dilemma posed by the public prestige and size of the independent sector in British education is acute. The public prestige is not altogether warranted. While a score or so of the most famous public schools unquestionably offer a very good, if traditional, education, there is a long 'tail' of poor and indifferent independent schools, trading on the snobbery of parents rather than on academic excellence. The independent sector underpins social as well as educational stratification; the boys and girls who attend independent schools, many of them boarding schools, rarely if ever encounter children from manual workers' homes. They have different accents, different behaviour and different experiences. Diversity is the lifeblood of pluralist societies; but sadly these diversities often mirror social divisions. Public school alumni move on into the better jobs society has to offer, exercising influence as managers, MPs, bankers and professionals – the officer class of the country; yet nothing in their lives will have made them familiar with the majority of those they seek to lead.

The maintained system of education and the economy itself are crippled by this socially segregated system. Yet in any democratic society, individual freedom of choice should be protected unless it interferes with the liberties or lives of others. It is with reluctance that I for one conclude that the freedom to send one's children to an independent school is bought at too high a price for the rest of society.

Any decision to prevent fee paying by law would have to be complemented by a major programme to integrate those independent schools who were willing into the maintained system. A number of them would be able to offer their experience as boarding schools for children whose family circumstances make boarding desirable. Others would become sixth-form colleges or upper secondary schools as did some of the direct-grant schools which entered the maintained system in 1976. Schools with a reputation for experiment could be offered as alternative schools within the state system in order to widen parental choice. Some schools would probably leave the country if fee paying was forbidden; but they would be much less influential in Eire or Switzerland than they are in England. If an imaginative range of ways to integrate independent schools could be found, many would decide to stay.

UNEQUAL OPPORTUNITIES

I said earlier in this chapter that much of the educational debate has been about systems rather than schools. Yet insistently at the heart of the educational debate is the question, what makes a good school? That question didn't seem to matter much in the late 1960s and early 1970s. Educational research both in the United States and in Britain concluded that the school was of no great significance either for the development of children or for offsetting social and environmental inequalities. Family background, parental attitudes, social class were all much more important. Christopher Jencks in his book *Inequality: a Re-assessment of the Effect of Family and Schooling in America*‡[2] declared firmly that 'equalizing the quality of high schools would reduce cognitive inequality by 1 per cent or less'.

James Coleman, in a highly influential report on *The Equality of Educational Opportunity*,[3] said that 'schools are successful only insofar as they reduce the dependence of a child's opportunities upon his social origins'. In the United States, where large sums of money had been ploughed into schools by the federal government under Title One of the Elementary and Secondary Education Act, 1965, and into compensatory education through the Headstart programme, disillusionment was widespread. 'Put crudely, the federal government was trying to buy improved academic performance, but it was not clear what commodity it was purchasing or what currency was legal tender in the transaction ... Not surprisingly, the consequent distress when academic performance did not improve challenged American faith in schooling.' So wrote Professor Patricia Graham in *Whither Equality of Educational Opportunity?* in February 1980.[4] But the dismissal of the influence of schools on children's life chances was too abrupt. In England, Michael Rutter stated, on the basis of his study of twelve London secondary schools, 'Schools do indeed have an important impact on children's development and it does matter which school a child attends.' His summary of conclusions began: 'Secondary schools in inner London differ markedly in the behaviour and attainments shown by their pupils. This was evident in the children's behaviour whilst at school ... the regularity of their attendance, the proportions staying on at school beyond the legally enforced period, their success in public examinations, and their delinquency rates.'[5] Rutter and his colleagues found that these variations held good even when comparisons were restricted to children with similar family backgrounds and personal characteristics prior to entering secondary school. The school itself made a difference – and a marked one.

Research on Title One of the Elementary and Secondary Education Act in the United States, undertaken by the National Institute of Education in 1974, also cast doubt on the sweeping conclusions of the Coleman Report and on those of Christopher Jencks and Arthur Jensen. Title One money *did* benefit pupils and improve their academic achievements *if* instructional programmes were well planned and well implemented – or, to put it plainly, if the pupils were well taught.

The school cannot on its own outweigh the powerful influences of social background, parental attitudes, and racial or sex discrimination, but it can significantly influence a child's development in spite of them. That schools do affect academic attainment, behaviour and social adjustment is now well attested. There are, of course, other influences unrelated to background or heredity that bear upon children – peer group attitudes, the impact of television and the commercial youth culture for instance; for otherwise how can one explain the fact that reading standards in primary schools both in the United States and in Britain have reached historically high levels, while tests of reading and mathematical ability taken at thirteen or seventeen show a decline, at least in the United States, and the results of US standard achievement tests (SATs) for entry into higher education have fallen for twenty years?

Whatever schools may do, unequal opportunities exist at, or even before, birth. Illegitimate children of teenage mothers or children born into large families are likely to be more sickly and are more often slow learners than children born into a small prosperous family. The correlation between the occupation or education of the parent(s) and the academic attainment of the child is high in all countries. Children from the inner cities are low achievers. In the United States the variation in mathematical test scores of nine-year-old children in 1978 averaged 15 per cent between the children of college and university educated parents and those whose parents had not graduated from high school. Nine-year-olds from disadvantaged urban backgrounds were 17 per cent behind those from the wealthy suburbs.[6]

Efforts to redress inequality have to be made much earlier in the child's life, and have to go far beyond education. Good maternity services, including pre- and postnatal care, are the first essential. The health and personal social services for the pre-school child should be linked closely to nursery education. That will require cooperation at local authority level between social service committees and education committees. Nursery schools have mainly benefited the middle class in Britain, partly because their sessions are too short to meet the needs of working mothers. Nursery schools should become the hub of a whole group of services for the young child, including health visitors, child care workers, mother-and-baby clinics, and resource and advice centres for nursery nurses and baby-minders and for parents themselves. The most disadvantaged parents will not come to a nursery school, so the nursery school has to find ways of reaching them. Health visitors have that kind of access. Once parents are used to taking their children to a nursery centre for a variety of services, it becomes easier to identify handicaps at an early stage. Far too many children are well into the primary school before handicaps are identified.

Early education can help to offset the disadvantages of family and social background, as Headstart has shown in the United States, but only if the compensatory elements of extra teaching and extra resources are sustained for several years. Children who are subjected to short bouts of extra coaching in reading or calculation may show an immediate improvement but then fall back again. At every stage of education, disadvantaged children need special help with language difficulties or learning difficulties. In the United States, Congress in 1978 voted for the integration of handicapped children into normal schools and laid it down that each child should have an individual learning programme. Individual learning programmes might help children disadvantaged in other ways as well, and would encourage schools to maintain records of the child's achievements and problems which could be handed on at each stage of the child's schooling. Such individual care has of course implications for the number and the skills of the teachers employed.

Parents' attitudes are a significant factor in children's achievements at school. There has been a remarkable improvement in the links between schools and parents in the last few years. Most schools now hold open evenings for parents to come and discuss their children's progress. Parents have much easier access to teachers, and some schools encourage them to visit whenever they want. Others use parents as helpers, especially with sports, crafts, reading and domestic science. Governing bodies of schools have parent representatives, and few schools are without a parent-teachers' association. But once again, it is the parents of the most disadvantaged children who rarely come to these functions. So teachers or educational welfare workers may have to make home visits and win parents' confidence. Where parents belong to an ethnic minority, they may be wary of unfamiliar authority, represented by the school. Counsellors of the same ethnic background can be very valuable in reaching these parents. In Cologne, Turkish counsellors, working with a German colleague, have been able to win the cooperation of Turkish parents on such delicate matters as the vocational education of girls. In Coventry, visits from West Indian and Asian teachers and counsellors have overcome the isolation of ethnic-minority parents. Community schools, offering access to libraries, sports facilities and classes for those of all generations, should improve parental attitudes too.

WHAT MAKES A GOOD SCHOOL?

What *does* make a good school? It has many ingredients: the school's objectives; relations between teachers and the head teacher or the school's administrators; the attitude of teachers to children and the extent of parental support for the school and the children; the age of the school buildings and the quality of its equipment, though they are less important than the teachers. In other words, resources help, but they are by no means the only important factor.

High professional standards on the part of teachers matter a lot, for teachers set the examples children model themselves upon. Schools can be traditional or progressive in their attitudes towards uniforms, prefects, methods of instruction or the use of Christian names between teachers and pupils. But if they accept classes that start late or end early, absenteeism among teachers or pupils for no good reason, little or no preparation of lessons and uncorrected homework, then the schools' standards begin to slip. The children will do as the teachers do.

The expectations that teachers have of their pupils exercise an important influence. Children tend to live up or down to expectations. It isn't surprising that children of above-average ability do less well in secondary modern schools than in grammar schools. The children themselves, like their parents and their teachers, *expect* to do less well; after all, they weren't selected so they can't be clever. Girls rarely choose to study science and mathematics, especially in mixed schools. They have learned to believe that girls are unsuited to science and mathematics, so they avoid them. Yet there are wide variations between countries, which suggests that the explanation is to be found in social attitudes rather than in biology. Teachers can overcome prejudices of these kinds by building up the confidence of their pupils; they can also confirm them by consciously or unconsciously adjusting their expectations and opinions of children to conform to the conventional view.

Educators tend to shy away from the question of what makes a good school, although if the answer could be found, the effect on making children's life chances more equal would be considerable. Educators shy away because some of the responses may be uncomfortable for them. For instance, the character and personality of the head teacher is the single most important factor in what makes a good school, at least in Britain where the head has so much power. The professional standards of the teaching staff and their concern for their pupils are very important too. The professional capacities of head and assistant teacher alike can certainly be enhanced by regular in-service training. In-service training is essential if teachers are to keep abreast of the latest thinking and developments in their subjects as well as new teaching methods. Teachers may serve for forty years after qualifying. They can easily pass on outdated or even incorrect information to their pupils if they are not given the opportunity to bring their own knowledge up to date. Good teachers eagerly take advantage of in-service training. Poor teachers often don't. Regular in-service training should be a requirement for promotion, provided the opportunity is generally available. Universities and polytechnics should willingly make such courses available, as well as the schools themselves offering school-based and school-focused in-service training. More effective induction of new teachers, with a reduction in their teaching load, and training in management for potential heads and deputy heads will also make schools better.

But the nasty question of what is to be done with poor head teachers or inadequate assistant teachers cannot be evaded. If they cannot reach a reasonable standard in their jobs, then they should not stay in the profession, though means should be found to ease their path out of it.

Politicians shy away from the question of what makes a good school because they prefer to explain things in terms of systems. It makes reform so much simpler. Stay with selective schools and standards will be high. Go comprehensive and give your children a better chance. But system changes only take one part of the way to success. The rest depends on the people in the school, on the human factor, just as it does with nationalized industries or governments or local authorities.

THE CURRICULUM

It is not only the schools themselves that matter, however, but what goes on in them, the content of the curriculum. The curriculum review launched in 1977 by the education ministers for England and Wales showed how little local education authorities knew about what was being taught in their schools, although they were legally responsible for the curriculum. In some districts, only one foreign language was offered; in others, children could not study single sciences, which is essential if they are to be taken to an advanced level. Everywhere, the curriculum was under pressure, with constant demands for additional fields of study, and equally continuous clamour for more time to be spent on basic skills.

We need to stand back a little and ask what kind of education the majority of children will need in the modern industrial world and in the post-industrial world, the information society. No one can say for sure. But where technological change is rapid, a broad foundation on which different skills can be built offers the soundest answer. Men and women will have to understand the new technologies well enough to be able to participate in sensible decisions about how they are to be used and for what ends. So the citizens of our democracies will need at least a nodding acquaintance with computers, microprocessors and technology more generally. They should be able to use mathematics as they can use language, that is be basically numerate as well as basically literate. And they will need to know enough about economics and the society of which they are part, nationally and internationally, to contribute to the new structures of industrial democracy and the participatory bodies in the schools and the other social institutions.

Children also have to be prepared for the social changes in modern society. Even if long periods of unemployment can be avoided, hours of work are likely to be shorter and holidays longer. People will want to be educated to use their leisure time enjoyably, to be able to exploit the opportunities open to them according to their individual choices. The emergence of women as equal citizens (and high unemployment could seriously prejudice its evolution) implies a fairer distribution of domestic and family responsibilities between men and women. This has clear consequences for the curriculum, some of them already being recognized in that subjects like domestic science and woodwork are now being taught both to boy and to girls.

In any educational structure dominated by public examinations, like that of Britain (and those of most of Western Europe), the curriculum can be reformed only if the examinations are reformed too. So a broadly based secondary curriculum, in which most subjects have to be taken by all children up to the age of sixteen, will require that the examinations themselves offer fewer options or, in other words, that the examinations cease to require such early choices of the subjects in which the children will specialize. In Britain it is possible for a pupil to concentrate exclusively on science subjects or on arts subjects from the age of sixteen or even younger. He or she need not offer mathematics or English, let alone science or a foreign language. It is a narrow base for the country's future leaders in management, the civil service and the professions, too narrow a base given the areas in which major changes are occurring. So the A level examinations also should be broadened; the proposals for two subsidiary subjects and three main subjects, and for one or more of these subjects to come from a different set of disciplines, deserve to be carefully considered.

THINKERS AND MAKERS

A broadening of the curriculum will only influence tangentially the most acute division of all in education, the split between academic and vocational education. Vocational education everywhere in Europe has long been the form of further education reserved for the socially inferior. Bright working-class boys got apprenticeships. Bright middle-class boys went to university. Until this generation, few girls did either. The massive expansion of higher education in the last thirty years has enabled far more bright working-class boys and girls of all social backgrounds to go on to higher education. But they are still only a small fraction of the total, at most one in four (Britain, as it happens, has the highest proportion of working-class youngsters in higher education of any Western European country, but that proportion hasn't changed in twenty years). Few middle-class young people take apprenticeships, though graduate unemployment has persuaded some to do so in Denmark and West Germany. Generally speaking, the two tracks remain separate and there is little intermeshing between them. Yet the divorce between the thinkers and the makers, those that study and those that do, is one of the most profound sources of social difference and influences society's attitudes towards manufacturing industry as against the professions. Victorian England's distaste for those in trade as distinct from gentlemen and scholars is embedded deep in the educational system, not only in England.

This traditional division has had serious consequences for society. It also has inconvenient consequences for the individual. Academically trained people rarely know how to maintain a car or mend the plumbing; some cannot even change a fuse. They are dependent on servants who no longer exist, or on uncertain and expensive repair services. A greater element of practical education in schooling at every level would prepare people to live more satisfying and independent lives.

It is the segregation between thinkers and makers that Sweden and Denmark are now tackling in their upper secondary schools, trying to bring together in one place vocational courses and academic courses, and allowing young people to put together combinations of both. It isn't only physical integration that is needed, however. Attainment in vocational courses should be recognized as a qualification for entry to higher education just as A levels are. Admittedly it is possible to enter university for a first degree course on the basis of an Ordinary National Certificate or Diploma, but very few do so. The government of France decided in 1976 to recognize technological qualifications – roughly the French equivalent of the Higher National Diploma – not only for entry to higher education, but also to the prestigious *grandes écoles*, including the École Nationale d'Administration, which leads to the highest posts in the French civil service. Despite this revolutionary step, French upper secondary education is still divided between academically oriented schools and technically oriented schools; the Scandinavians have gone much further.

Vocational education in Britain, as in France, is largely segregated into separate institutions, the colleges of further education, while the school sixth forms concentrate on academic studies. But there has been a gradual coming together. Further education colleges offer academic courses to their students in a wide range of subjects. Sixth forms have begun to add technical courses and business courses for the 'non-academic sixth' – youngsters who stay on for a year or even two to get professional qualifications.

The most highly integrated combination of academic and vocational education is found in the tertiary colleges, which take in all the sixteen-year-olds in a particular area, whether they intend to take vocational subjects, academic subjects, or a combination of both, and whether they are full-time or part-time. The opportunities for students to mix socially and in extra-curricular activities make traditional distinctions between vocational and academic seem absurd; each group learns something about the work of the other.

Given the extreme pressures on financial resources, a national network of tertiary colleges is unlikely to be achieved for many years to come; however, other areas have sixth-form colleges or community schools, which can help to bridge the divide between vocational and academic education.

The sixth-form college can offer a combined range of courses alongside the further education college, allowing students to take some courses in one institution and some in the other. Sixth forms in schools can do the same, though their much more limited size makes timetabling difficult. The sixth-form college can open its doors to adult students who would like to study a particular subject, since most student groups are small and teachers can easily manage a few additional students. Community schools, one of the most exciting recent developments in British education, already include adult students in many of their classes, though some limit their participation to classes outside school hours, or to classes in subjects such as art, metalwork and pottery. The community school means what its name says; its facilities are shared with the local neighbourhood, it is open from early in the morning until late at night, and it is part of the community rather than separated from it, as so many traditional secondary schools still are.

Yet many of these traditional secondary schools are embracing new commitments to the community too. As pupil numbers fall, and they will fall by a third in the secondary schools in the present decade, empty classrooms are being used for nursery groups or for classes for the young unemployed. Declining numbers make life very difficult for schools, especially if financial resources are cut correspondingly; but they do offer opportunities too, providing spare space and available teaching capacity if used with imagination.

One problem in bringing vocational education and academic education closer together is the separate salary scales, different working conditions and sometimes different qualifications required of teachers. Everywhere in Western Europe these differences have made integration difficult. In Britain, the Burnham negotiations for school teachers are conducted separately from those for college teachers and salary structures are quite distinct. Bringing salary structures, regulations and requirements together is a tedious job, but it is essential if the two strands of education, academic and vocational, are at last to be integrated.

The system of educational grants in England and Wales has encouraged academically able boys and girls from working-class homes to attend universities and polytechnics once they have struggled through A levels, but it does nothing to help them get that far. Grants for young people between the ages of sixteen and nineteen are discretionary (each local authority decides whether or not to give them) and often derisory. Young people can draw benefit if unemployed; they can get a training allowance on a work experience course or a short industrial course run by the Manpower Services Commission. But if they stay on at school voluntarily or attend a college of further education full-time, they receive no grant, or at most a nominal discretionary one, however small the family income. Not only does the system encourage young people from less well-off homes to leave full-time education at the earliest legal age; it also deprives the country of many potentially qualified people.

The distinction continues into higher education, where full-time students on degree courses get mandatory grants and part-time students and those studying for qualifications other than degrees get nothing, or at best a small discretionary grant. Proposals to start a pilot scheme for means-tested grants for the full-time education of sixteen- to nineteen-year-olds were shelved when the Labour government fell in 1979 so the necessary shake-up in the grants system has been postponed yet again.

HIGHER EDUCATION

The repercussions of integrating vocational and academic education involve higher education too. The division between the universities and the polytechnics, the 'binary system', was established in 1967 by Anthony Crosland, then the Secretary of State for Education and Science, in order to encourage the polytechnics to be very different institutions from the universities. He wanted them to attract mature students, part-time students and students studying for qualifications other than degrees, and he hoped that they would identify with their local communities, since they would be financed largely from local government sources and not by the University Grants Commission. But the polytechnics, like their predecessors, the colleges of advanced technology, have been attracted by the university model. While they retain some differences, particularly a greater emphasis on technology, their student bodies resemble those of the universities in having a preponderance of young men and women studying full-time for a first degree.

As the number of undergraduate students falls through the late 1980s, both the universities and the polytechnics will have an opportunity to widen their intake. The polytechnics, unlike most universities, have catered for part-time students to some extent, but there is plenty of scope for attracting more mature students, students on in-service and refresher courses and those studying at home for short residential periods.

While formal higher education in Britain has been succoured with very high staff–student ratios of under one in ten, and reasonably generous financing, adult education has never got away from its earnest evening-class image. The life of an adult student, full or part-time, is harsh, and little provision is made for him or her in the formal system. The existing university system has about one in ten students aged over twenty-four, and few part-timers. Summer courses for those who want a short period of intensive education are rare, apart from conferences and the Open University's residential courses, themselves an innovation. If the Open University, the further education colleges and the resources of the higher education system were brought together, a system of continuing education could be established in Britain. It would require the cooperation of the universities. The institutions of higher education in Britain do not see themselves as resource centres for their own cities or counties in the way that American universities do. But there need be no tension between this role and the role of being internationally recognized centres of academic excellence. The University of California at Berkeley, for instance, manages both without damaging its reputation.

The reforms proposed in the public examination system would entail a less specialized first degree course, as universities are quick to point out. The more specialized courses would then have to be taken at postgraduate level, as they are in the United States, and there would have to be more 'taught' postgraduate courses, which might be no bad thing. Broader first degree courses would fit in to the requirements of the new society. Many of the new developments require several disciplines to be brought together. Biotechnology, for instance, involves biologists, chemists, chemical engineers, biochemists, molecular biologists and electronic engineers working together. Because of the high degree of specialization in science, such cooperation isn't easy. Microelectronics will, as we have seen, affect a huge range of activities from schoolteaching to engineering maintenance. The men and women educated in a narrow specialism will find it difficult to adapt to the change. As for the civil service, into which so many of the more able graduates go, would it not benefit from the entry of young men and women with at least a rudimentary knowledge of science and technology as well as of philosophy, history and politics?

12

Political Institutions

Institutional factors are often singled out as being more important than anything else in explaining the crisis of Western society, and of all our institutions it is political institutions that have been most sharply criticized. Their alleged remoteness, their bureaucracy, their conservatism and their incompetence have been attacked by both left and right, and by the adherents of a very varied assortment of doctrines: monetarists, Marxists, utopians, ecologists, authoritarians and anarchists among them.

Among the less politically active public too there has in recent years been evidence of declining confidence and trust. This declining trust is obviously correlated with governments' lack of success in achieving the goals of economic growth and a better standard of living which they have publicly set for themselves; many people accuse them of 'broken promises'. But governments have not tried less hard to achieve these goals in the 1970s and 1980s than in the 1950s or 1960s; the goals have proved elusive because of the massive change of external circumstances outlined in Chapter 4 of this book. Governments are more to be blamed for failing to admit or even to see that circumstances have changed radically, and that traditional policies cannot be pursued successfully in those changed circumstances, than for lack of commitment or effort.

In a seminal book, first published in 1962, *The Structure of Scientific Revolutions*,[1] Thomas Kuhn described how natural scientists work within a paradigm – that is to say a universally accepted framework of thought which in effect determines the kinds of questions they ask and the kinds of answers they provide. Within the currently accepted paradigm scientific knowledge is cumulative, adding to the sum of information and resolving outstanding problems. But then anomalies emerge which cannot be resolved in terms of the paradigm. Copernicus could not fit his observations into Ptolemy's description of the universe, although Ptolemy's laws had reigned unchallenged for centuries. Similarly, Einstein could not fit relativity into Newton's assumptions about space and time. So the anomalies became the basis of a challenge to the old assumptions, the traditional paradigm. Out of the challenge emerged a new paradigm, the result of a revolution in scientific thinking.

Kuhn draws a parallel with political institutions:

Political revolutions are inaugurated by a growing sense, often restricted to a segment of the political community, that existing institutions have ceased adequately to meet the problems posed by the environment that they have in part created. In much the same way, scientific revolutions are inaugurated by a growing sense, again often restricted to a narrow subdivision of the scientific community, that an existing paradigm has ceased to function adequately in the exploration of an aspect of nature to which that paradigm itself had previously led the way. In both political and scientific development the sense of malfunction that can lead to crisis is prerequisite to revolution.[2]

The analogy can be reversed. The governments of advanced industrial societies today behave rather like alchemists. Alchemists laboured mightily to find a formula that would transmute other materials into gold. Having at best a patchy understanding of chemistry they did not realize that gold could not be made from these materials; in short, they were working with the wrong set of assumptions, the wrong paradigm.

The governments of the advanced industrial societies are likewise working, so it seems to me, on a wrong set of assumptions. They cannot get back to full employment or humane social services or good industrial relations on the present basis. Like the alchemists, they will find out that no amount of painstaking effort will change dross into gold. The effort should be directed instead to explanation and education, to presenting honestly to the public how circumstances have changed, what the new range of choices is, and what are the policies that governments are capable of carrying out. Future promises will have to be fewer and less sweeping.

Sometimes there will be warnings rather than promises. But political institutions based on realistic assumptions will at least recover some of their credibility, and credibility is essential to the democratic process.

CRISIS OF CONFIDENCE

In the English-speaking countries, the crisis of confidence in political institutions has been expressed in negative rather than in positive terms. Many voters have simply not bothered to vote. In the last off-year US Congressional election in 1978 (when there was no election for President), 45.9 per cent of the adult population cast a vote. In the presidential election of November 1980, only 52 per cent of eligible adults voted. Voting participation has declined in the US in the last fifteen years, although television has given presidential and congressional candidates far greater opportunities to be seen and recognized by voters than their predecessors enjoyed, and although levels of general education have continued to rise.

While general elections attract much higher participation from British voters than do presidential elections from American voters, in Britain too the proportion of the electorate who bother to vote has declined. In May 1979, 76 per cent voted, slightly better than in October 1974, but below the turn-outs at elections in the early 1950s; in 1950, 84 per cent of the electorate voted. In both the United States and in Britain, enthusiasm for voting is considerably stronger among the middle-aged and elderly than among voters under twenty-five. In Britain in 1979, voting among those over sixty outnumbered voting amongst those under twenty-five by at least five percentage points and probably more. In 1978, fewer than one in four American voters aged under twenty-four went to cast their vote for a candidate for Congress. The scepticism of British voters towards their political system is rather more obvious when one looks at the votes cast for the two major parties. (Though dominated by the Labour and Conservative parties since 1945, British politics has never been an exclusively two-party system. The Liberal party has offered an alternative choice in many constituencies, and in Scotland, Wales and Northern Ireland there have been nationalist alternatives as well. Extreme parties of the right and left have also put up candidates in what seemed to them promising constituencies, though none of these parties has had any formal representation in Parliament since 1951, nor more than a derisory vote.) The attitude of the electors to the two major parties seems lukewarm, especially if their share of the eligible electorate is taken, rather than their share of those who voted: 28 per cent of the electorate voted Labour in 1979; 33 per cent Conservative. So the Conservative government elected in 1979 was put in power by only a third of the adult population.

The evidence of disaffection as seen in elections is supported by responses to public opinion polls. The British public assess politicians as being in the most disreputable profession apart from journalism. Seventy per cent of a large sample tested in 1976 thought people in politics were habitual liars, and a majority saw them as acting on behalf of 'a few big interests'. This view was held about members of both major parties.[3]

Perhaps because of this cynical assessment, voters lose patience with the governments they elect much more quickly than they used to do. A new government's 'honeymoon period' is much shorter than in the past. For much of their time in office, recent British governments have governed without the support of even the biggest single body of prevailing opinion, let alone a majority.

Disillusionment with their political institutions seems to be less widespread but fiercer in other European countries. German electors still go to the polls in very large numbers, over 85 per cent voting in the October 1980 Federal elections. In France, 87 per cent of the electorate cast their vote in the final round of the presidential election in 1974, and 84 per cent also voted in the first round. But the existence of minorities passionately antagonistic to existing political institutions has been dramatically demonstrated in both countries. France has not wholly overcome the trauma of the 1968 student revolt, which failed because the students were unable to win the support of organized industrial workers. West Germany nervously searches the political undergrowth to see if the nihilism of the Baader-Meinhof group still germinates there. Signs of protest do not need to take such a menacing form, however. The 'green parties' on the continent of Europe, still small enough to be irritants rather than threats, are gaining members and votes, especially among young people, in spite of their unresolved internal conflicts.

SINGLE-ISSUE POLITICS

The burgeoning of single-issue politics, most strikingly in the United States, is another indication of the loss of faith in traditional political institutions. More and more candidates for Congress determine their chances of re-election not by adherence to a particular party, but by their attitudes on a small number of key issues. In the last few years, abortion, women's rights, and certain sensitive environmental issues such as civil nuclear power have made or unmade American politicians. In the elections of November 1980, a distinguished group of liberal-minded Senators, including George McGovern of South Dakota, Frank Church of Idaho and John Culver of Iowa, were swept out of office, not only because of the national swing to the Republicans, but also because they were marked out as victims by a number of single-issue groups. The passionate advocates of these single issues are rarely interested in a candidate's attitude towards the policy platform of his party. It is one issue and one issue alone that will determine their votes and perhaps their active support or hostility in the election.

Single-issue politics has been one of the main forces operating on the United States Congress, which has changed a great deal since the early 1970s. The system of seniority for committee chairmanships has been weakened and the chairman's position is much less powerful than it used to be. Committees and sub-committees have proliferated; their staffs have multiplied.

US administrations have never found it easy to get their proposals through Congress. The legislature pores over everything the administration does, and few proposals go through without being substantially altered or added to. Indeed, so great is the legislature's power that the administration will tack bits on to its legislative proposals for the sole purpose of winning the support of an influential Senator or Congressman. But, as a result of reforms in the last decade, the Congress has now become even stronger relative to the administration, and Congress's strength is in part the American political system's weakness. It is a strange strength, a strength to obstruct and deny rather than to propose and affirm.

The decline of party cohesion has been hastened by the end of the seniority system, and the reform of the primary system has largely removed the influence of the political machines, so that each candidate runs for himself or herself. 'Name recognition' is absolutely crucial in states where there is cross-voting at primaries, i.e. where voters registered with one party can vote in the primaries of the other. The decentralized pattern of the media, with separate local television stations in every community of any size, fragments politics further. It is the folks back home who make the crucial decisions on which candidates are chosen and who is then elected, not the party bosses in the state capitol, let alone Washington.

Strangely enough, this decentralization of political power has evolved alongside a massive bureaucratization of Congress. The paid professional staffs of Senators and Congressmen and of their committees, the lawyers, researchers and aides, increased from 980 in 1970 to over 13,000 in 1979. The professional staff is becoming a new mandarinate, with its own career structure (often leading on to elective positions), its own network of relationships and its own kinds of prestige. On most committees, professional aides can sit in for their elected masters as observers; on some, they can speak and ask questions. Congressmen are busy people, burdened by long journeys between their districts and Washington, beset by the demands of their constituents and under pressure to keep up with the work of large numbers of committees – those on which they do not sit as well as those on which they do. It is not surprising that some aides make their own mutual arrangements and deals. Professional aides are often recruited direct from among new university graduates and postgraduates, especially those from the more famous private institutions. Many are lawyers. They are beginning to form a new élite in American politics, an élite inevitably centred on Washington.

The legislature is not so much decentralized as fragmented. Administrations have tried to devolve some decision-making powers back to the states and the localities. President Nixon, for instance, switched funds for welfare and unemployment away from federal agencies into a system of grants for 'prime sponsors', which were either cities or groups of rural counties. But local devolution lives uneasily with congressional attempts to impose highly detailed accountability for federal spending. The outcome is all too often a mass of regulations that are either disregarded or bent to suit the prime sponsors' purpose.

A fragmented Congress is a Congress that finds unpopular decisions very hard to make, for each decision on each issue becomes part of the individual record the Congressman will have to defend at the next election, often to single-issue groups. He or she cannot hide beneath the mantle of party discipline, for it does not exist. Nor will the government fall if the Congressman refuses to support the President's proposals. So only very brave or very foolhardy Congressmen take unpopular stands. The economic and social climate for the industrial world is becoming harsher and will become harsher still. To adjust to that climate, governments will have to make painful and often unpopular decisions. In the United States it is difficult to see how such decisions can get through Congress, unless there is a change in the public mood or in the institutions themselves.

Single-issue politics has not wielded so much influence in Western European democracies. But even in Europe, there has been a significant increase in the number of people involved in voluntary organizations of a political character, and a significant decline in the numbers who are members of political parties. These voluntary organizations are concerned with political objectives, usually in a single area, such as nuclear power, overseas aid, famine relief, child poverty, preservation of the countryside, abortion, women's rights, civil liberties, stopping motorways, and unilateral nuclear disarmament. Very often the active campaigners have more sympathy for one party than another, because it seems likely to share their objectives. Yet most of these politically involved people stay out of party politics; some would hold party politics in contempt.

It is difficult to be sure, but there is considerable anecdotal evidence to suggest that many of those who are deeply involved in issue organizations, without being in any way active in party politics, are young people. Certainly the extreme protest movements such as the Red Brigades in Italy and Baader-Meinhof in West Germany are, or were, made up almost entirely of men and women in their twenties and thirties. Young people are better educated than their parents were, less resigned to injustices, much more conscious of their rights. There is no reason to believe that they are less politically minded. But for some reason, the traditional political parties do not appeal to them, or at least not very much.

Part of the explanation lies in the changes described in Chapter 4. Governments of all political persuasions have been less successful in improving people's standards of living, less successful in keeping prices down and employment up, than they were in the 1950s and 1960s. Their indifferent record has soured many voters, and led them to blame governments for circumstances often beyond government control. Yet it is not the whole story, for some of the most spectacular protests occurred in the late 1960s, when most Western governments were buoyed up by what appeared to be a permanently rising tide of prosperity. Furthermore, the drift away from the traditional parties started before the economic slowdown began.

THE TECHNOLOGICAL IMPERATIVE

In Chapter 8, I said that the two major British political parties moved down the same road of concentration together, even though they argued that the road was different. Certainly the parties disagreed strongly on where the border should lie between the public and private sectors. Certainly they differed on the proportion of the national income that should go to public expenditure and, within public expenditure, how much should go to defence and how much to education, health and personal social services. Certainly they had very different views on the respective importance of equality and of individual advancement. Yet both accepted the technological imperative, the dominance of the means of production over the quality of human life. If the means of production demanded large units, large units there would be, whatever the cost in job satisfaction or communication.

The unquestioning acceptance of economic and technological objectives, in particular economic growth at almost any social cost, is shared by the major political parties of the democratic West: it is also shared by the great monolithic parties of the Soviet bloc countries. Communist governments pursue economic growth even more single-mindedly than Western governments do. Targets are set, and there is great rejoicing in official circles if they are met or surpassed. Independent trade unions might hamper economic growth, so independent trade unions cannot be permitted – or only, as in Poland, if the alternative might be a popular uprising. Industry in Communist countries is subjected to less rigorous environmental regulation than it is in the United States or north-western Europe; the pollution of rivers, and indeed of the entire Caspian Sea, has become a question of international concern.

Sometimes the imperative of economic growth clashes with the political doctrines of Communism – the public ownership of the means of production, distribution and exchange, or the distribution of income on the grounds of need rather than ability or power. More and more frequently in the Communist countries, the political doctrine yields to the imperative of economic growth. Large loans are raised from the capitalist West. The privately owned sector grows, especially in agriculture. Income distribution becomes more unequal, and incomes are themselves enhanced by special privileges – priority in buying a car, access to shops selling imported goods or to better housing, permission to live in the metropolis rather than in the countryside. The People's Republic of China is a remarkable example of the objective of economic growth taking priority over doctrine. Talented young scientists and engineers are selected for special educational opportunities (as they are in the Soviet Union also), and are encouraged to pursue their higher studies in the capitalist world. Children of professional cadres and these professional groups themselves are no longer obliged to spend some years in manual work. China is even permitting the establishment of limited liability companies as an experiment.

To visit China is to visit a country enthralled by the prospect of modernization and anxious to adopt the best technologies the world can offer, whatever the source – and the source is often the United States, Japan or other capitalist countries. Nor are the leaders of China bothered about the social cost of introducing these technologies. In 1978 I asked the then Minister of Education how China would find employment for the hundreds of millions of Chinese employed on the land – and 80 per cent of the Chinese population is employed on the land – if agriculture was mechanized. He found the question a very odd one. Nowhere did the problem of the social costs of rapid industrialization really impinge.

Politicians find it odd when people respond to public opinion polls by saying they find no difference between the parties; or if the politicians claim to understand, they do so by arguing that the parties share too much of the centre ground. I suspect, however, that many young people simply regard the political parties as committed to 'the system'; not the capitalist system or the socialist system, but the industrial system, which spans both. Young people fail to vote in the West; they show evident boredom with politics in the East. Some in the Soviet bloc look longingly at the other half of the industrial world, at the greener fields where jeans are well cut, discos flourish and pop music is adventurous; some of their opposite numbers in the West believe they might achieve through Marxism a society without exploitation of man by man and without a ruling class, if only capitalism were overthrown. More and more young people, however, belong to a counter-culture which looks neither to capitalism nor to communism. Capitalist societies are run by a coalition of big government, big business and big unions. Communist societies are run just by big government, in which the different departments representing industrial, agricultural and labour interests fight their internal battles. Meanwhile members of the counter-culture, most of them young, explore alternative ways of living, work – often very hard – at what they choose to do, and reject the values of the large organizations. The traditional political parties say little that these people want to hear. Of course a political party's support may be enlisted for a particular purpose, such as saving whales from slaughter or legalizing abortion; but the party is seen as an instrument, not as a cause. Once again, it is the single issue that counts. I do not want to exaggerate the position. In Western European countries, most young people vote, and most vote in the same way as their parents. But the attitude of many young people, often the more articulate, is influenced by alienation from traditional industrial society, whatever the nominal ideology of that society may be.

The constitutional structures of Western European countries do not lend themselves to single-issue politics in the way the American structure does. For one thing, there are no primaries, so that voters cannot choose between the candidates of one party. For another, legislatures are much less powerful in Western Europe *vis-à-vis* the executive than in the United States and, perhaps partly for this reason, party cohesion is stronger. True, there has been some erosion of party discipline in Britain. Revolts by backbench Members of Parliament against government proposals are more frequent than they were, but they are almost always calculated to amend the proposals and not to threaten the government itself. Members of Parliament know that governments are elected on certain major policy proposals, and that governments, if defeated on them, have to resign. So backbench MPs may hail limited victories against the government of the day on school transport or on the allocation of jobs to dock-workers, but they know that victories against the government on the budget or on major legislation are not possible. Pressure on such matters must be exercised in advance, through the machinery of intra-party consultation. Governments will of course lose public support if they make unpopular decisions even if they retain their parliamentary support, but since the account is drawn up only at the end of the Parliament they do not have to deal with adverse votes day after day.

The danger to the British Parliament is not that it will obstruct the executive, but that it will seem irrelevant. Parliamentary debate is nowadays only one among many ways of informing and influencing public opinion, and certainly not the most widely disseminated one. Serving in Parliament has become a full-time occupation, and a rather better paid one, so more and more MPs are career politicians in the sense that their main commitment is to politics, and not to the law or agriculture or industry. MPs bring to Parliament less *outside* experience than they used to do, and the debates can be remote from the concerns of the general public.

SELECT COMMITTEES

Parliament has sought to compensate for the declining impact of debates by controlling the executive in other ways. The main means chosen has been the establishment of Select Committees to monitor each government department's activities. Select Committees have existed for many years. The Public Accounts Committee was set up in 1861, the Select Committee on Estimates, later replaced by the Select Committee on Expenditure, in 1912. Both these committees act as parliamentary watchdogs over the expenditure of monies voted by Parliament. But the detailed examination of the work of every government department is something new. A limited experiment, covering six departments, was started in 1966. Backbench pressure for an extension to all government departments was recognized by the Conservative government elected in 1979, which agreed to the setting up of Select Committees for all departments in its first parliamentary session. The committees were nominated in November 1979.

The Select Committees do not enjoy the huge staffs of congressional committees. Most have only half a dozen professional staff members. Nor can Members of Parliament be represented on the committees by their aides, even where they have them. The Select Committees, nevertheless, have proved to be energetic, controversial and determined. They have laid about them vigorously, insisting on calling witnesses, demanding information, protesting when papers are withheld and criticizing government departments in outspoken terms. Members of Parliament from both major parties have sometimes agreed about the committees' strictures on government departments. The legislature may begin to find as much solidarity in its criticisms of the executive as the parties have found in their battles with one another.

Have the Select Committees had any impact on public disillusionment with political institutions? The answer cannot be given yet. But some of the voluntary organizations with political objectives are beginning to advocate their cases to the Select Committees, thus gradually re-integrating themselves into the political process.

The Select Committees may perform another very important function, that of making the corporate bodies more accountable for what they do. For in the coalition of large corporate powers, only government is accountable to Parliament, and through Parliament to the people, for what it does. Neither industry, the professions nor the trade unions are subject to the same kind of scrutiny. The Select Committees, by inviting evidence from industry, the trade unions and the professions, not just on what these want but on the degree of cooperation they are prepared to offer in furthering various policies and various reforms, could be an important way of asserting the wider public interest.

The press have shown much less interest in the influence on policy-making of the social partners, industry, the trade unions and the professional organizations, than in that of politicians. Yet the influence wielded by these institutions is greater than that of all but the Cabinet itself and of a few powerful individual ministers and of course the Prime Minister. In some instances, their influence can be greater than that of Parliament itself. The press and television are fascinated by personalities, so their coverage of leading politicians is intense. The social partners, like the executive departments, attract far less attention. Clashes between the House of Commons and the government, especially revolts led by prominent backbenchers of the government party, are closely followed and reported, but the pressures from interests behind the scenes, often more effective in altering government policies, go largely unnoticed. One reason for this is secrecy about the governing process in Britain and the paucity of studies about how government departments operate and what determines the decisions they take.

In theory, ministers are responsible to Parliament for everything that happens in their departments. Cabinet ministers share collective responsibility for the actions of the government, whether or not those actions relate to the Cabinet minister's own department. These are the central constitutional doctrines of Cabinet government, together with the dependence of the Cabinet on the support of Parliament, without which it cannot continue to govern.

THE CHARACTERISTICS OF GOVERNMENT DEPARTMENTS

In practice, ministers cannot possibly control or even know about everything that happens in their departments. If it was ever the case that they did, the growth of government in the past hundred years now makes ministerial responsibility in that sense impossible. Government departments evolve their own ways of working and their own relationship with interest groups, and to a great extent these characteristics do not alter as governments come and go. Indeed, it is hard to see how government departments could administer the areas for which they are responsible if they had to change completely every time the government did. Departments develop a character of their own. This is formed partly by their last great achievement or reform. Thus, the Department of Health and Social Security is proud of the National Health Service and has a departmental loyalty towards it. It is likely to defend it against its detractors. The Department of Education and Science, when I first was a minister there in 1967, was still marked by the selective and meritocratic values of the 1944 Education Act, the most important educational milestone of the century up to then. Gradually the Department moved towards supporting the reform of secondary schools on comprehensive lines. Comprehensive reorganization replaced selective secondary education as the banner round which the Department rallied.

The character of departments is not established only by their greatest achievements, however. It is also formed by their relationships with the particular interest groups with which they normally work. The Department of Employment, for instance, tends to be close to and sympathetic towards the trade unions. The Department of Industry hears a lot about the problems of business and is close to the Confederation of British Industry. Both Departments are more favourable to protectionist policies than, say, the Foreign Office or the Department of Trade. The danger is that departments will get too close to their particular interest groups, to the point of advocating their interests against the interests of the wider community. Agricultural departments, for instance, often seem much more concerned about farmers' interests than about consumers' interests. Industrial departments tend to be soft on monopolies and mergers, even though the wider public interest may suffer.

Close relationships over a period between the senior civil servants in a department and their related client groups or interest groups are likely to build up mutual understanding and even mutual support. Furthermore, going along with the wishes of the interest groups makes for a much easier life. The safeguard for the public interest lies in scrutiny by Parliament and the media, for without such scrutiny there is a real danger of a cosy conspiracy between the coalition of corporate interests and the executive.

OPEN GOVERNMENT

The Select Committees are excellent instruments for exploring the policy-making of departments, and the relationship between departments and interest groups, provided they avoid the mistake of creating their own alternative and highly politicized civil service as the congressional committees have done. But they need a more open climate in which to flourish. It is high time that Parliament put a freedom of information Act on the statute book, limiting classification of documents to matters of state security, defence strategy, commercial secrecy and information that might directly harm individuals, for instance personal files. There must also be a body independent of government to scrutinize decisions about classification, for it is likely that many documents would be classified as secret unnecessarily if such an Act were passed. The powers of the Parliamentary Commissioner could be extended to adjudicate on the classification of documents, since his duty is to represent the interest of the public; but it could also be done, much less satisfactorily in my view, by a committee of Privy Councillors or even by the courts. Cabinet minutes should not be made public, since Cabinet government stands and falls on collective responsibility; publication of minutes would start off irresistible pressures to discover who stood where on what. But there is no reason why all the papers going to the Cabinet should be kept secret. Those from the Central Policy Review Staff should inform and enlighten public and parliamentary debate. Nor is there any reason why the membership or the existence of Cabinet committees should be concealed.

Open government would impinge on the way government departments are administered. In 1977, following widespread concern in the press and elsewhere about the education system, in which the Prime Minister had himself intervened, I decided to hold a series of regional conferences on various aspects of education – the curriculum, the question of standards, the training of teachers and the links between education and the world of work. A wide range of people was invited, including representatives of teachers, of parents, of industry, of trade unions, of local education authorities and of the pupils themselves. The experiment was regarded in some quarters as a gimmick. But in fact it allowed ministers to explain their problems and priorities to a wider interested public. The conferences revealed more confidence in the schools than the press campaign had suggested; and a more balanced and friendly atmosphere in which to advance proposals for reform was created. In the Department of Energy, Tony Benn convened a public conference on energy policy, in which he and his colleagues put forward their proposals. In a relatively homogeneous, unified state like Britain, such experiments in public participation are not difficult to mount.

Government in Britain is honeycombed with jobs, most of them prestigious but unpaid, as members of advisory or consultative committees. There are also posts that are powerful and command reasonable salaries, for instance the chairmen and board members of nationalized industries. These posts are in the gift of ministers, advised by their civil servants. But why should they not be openly advertised and filled after interview by a panel which would, for the more important posts, include a minister? I recall instituting this procedure for the post of Director-General of Fair Trading when I was Secretary of State for Prices and Consumer Protection. It was a radical departure and has been followed in only a very few instances. Yet it is one way to break through and widen the closed circle of government in Britain.

There are other needed reforms as well – many more exchanges between industry, local government and the civil service; a requirement that all administrators should from time to time in their careers deal directly with the public their department affects; greater recruitment of older entrants with experience in the outside world; an end to the traditional division between the scientific and technical civil service and the administrative and executive civil service. Such changes would narrow the gap between the civil service and the public it deals with, and would widen participation in the process of government. The real key to wider participation, however, lies in the devolution of decision-making from the centre, both by government and also by the social partners.

I have already attempted to describe how decision-making might be widened in industry and in the social services to include those the decisions affect. In education, students as well as teachers in colleges and universities have had some voice in decision-making since 1968. Involving parents – and older pupils – in the government of schools has been a slower and more difficult process, not least because local authorities have been reluctant to yield control of governing bodies. Obviously the limits of responsibility and of accountability must be defined as clearly as possible so that decisions are not the subject of demarcation disputes. Within those limits, however, the works committee or the school governing body must be free to reach its own decisions; beyond them, it can only express a view.

Government has to accept the parallel devolution of decision-making to local and regional authorities. Britain is an over-governed country, and three tiers should suffice: local, regional and national. Since constant upheaval worsens the quality of administration, the first steps might be to bring together the existing county and metropolitan authorities in each region on a consultative basis, as at present happens in Regional Economic Planning Councils. Scotland has its own legal system, so the case for the Scottish Grand Committee's work being done by a Scottish Assembly is very strong. English legislation on partially devolved subjects like education is likely to remain with the House of Commons. Where any such subject falls to the Scottish Assembly in Scotland, Members representing Scottish seats should not vote on it in the Commons.

To conclude, a successful democracy needs open discussion involving as many groups of concerned and interested people as possible. Policy makers should be willing to see new proposals put forward and publically discussed on the basis of the knowledge and information now available only to the government. Certain information must be kept secret for legitimate reasons, but secrecy in Britain goes beyond necessity to embrace the convenience of the governors, both elected and appointed, in avoiding detailed scrutiny of their decisions. So Britain needs a freedom of information Act, enough expert staff (but not too many) to enable Select Committees to monitor and examine government departments effectively, and a civil service much more ready to recruit from, and move into, the world outside.

CONTINUITY

What bedevils British government is the lack of continuity, even for those fields of policy-making where it is essential and where the lead times for investment or development far exceed the period of a single Parliament. Industrial investment, energy planning and educational policy changes are all examples of areas where decisions take anything up to ten or fifteen years to bear fruit. In contemporary Britain, policies that might be beneficial and new agencies or institutions that perform valuable roles are discarded, distorted or broken simply because a government other than that of the party now in power introduced them. The Industrial Reconstruction Corporation and the National Enterprise Board are both instances of useful bodies destroyed or crippled by successor governments. Over the exhausted body of British industry the political battle rages on.

There are strongly held differences of principle between parties, which must be expressed and acted upon. But there are also differences of opinion based on inexperience and on ignorance. Sadly, governments often learn in their last two or three years much that their successors will painfully and expensively learn all over again. Is there any way that this experience and knowledge can be conveyed from government to government, though each may represent a different party?

The Select Committees offer some hope here, as Members of Parliament begin to know a department well and to convey to ministers their own proposals and observations about it, sometimes across party lines. Greater awareness of the social partners will help. I would advocate in addition that no legislation should in future be presented to Parliament without first being discussed in draft form with the appropriate Select Committee. In the case of significant legislation the main changes proposed should be set out in a Green Paper to be debated by the House of Commons as well as within the Select Committee before legislation is introduced. Not only would such a reform provide greater continuity; it would also increase the legislature's influence over the executive.

Any democracy tending towards the pattern of a corporate state, as most Western European democracies are doing, badly needs parliamentary and media interest in the other organizations that wield power in the state. There are some indications that a more profound analysis of industry and trade unions is emerging in the press and the other media, though so strong is the cult of political personalities that leaders of the great corporate powers rarely get the coverage accorded to politicians.

At the other end of the spectrum, the United States and Canada are threatened with fragmentation rather than with corporatism. It is hard to see how the genie that has emerged can be forced back into the bottle. Tighter restrictions over the financing of American elections might reduce the power of single-issue groups. Congress may become jealous of the intrusions of non-elected staff into the power constitutionally accorded to elected representatives. More radically, the fixed term of the two houses of Congress might be replaced by a presidential power to dissolve one or both of them, a power possessed by the French President. Each side of the Atlantic looks longingly at the strengths of the other side's system; each is conscious of the limitations of its own.

In Western Europe, support for reversing the tide of centralized national power is growing. The movement is ardent in Spain and is beginning to emerge in France, both unitary states, as well as Britain. It is obvious in Canada. The nation-state, which has dominated the history of the nineteenth and twentieth centuries, is being pulled apart by centrifugal pressures, pressures for power to be devolved downwards to regional and local government, pressures for power to be transferred upwards to international and supranational bodies. The nation-state can yield a good deal of power without threatening its own survival, and in so doing, can help to create a better fit between institutions and their functions in the modern post-industrial world.

13

The Third World and Europe: Challenge and Response

The last twenty years have been years in which scores of countries have become independent nations, escaping from the bonds of the old European empires of Britain, France, Portugal and Spain. Yet paradoxically nations lead less and less autonomous existences. Political independence is not synonymous with economic or cultural or military independence. Indeed, independence is a misleading term to describe the position even of the superpowers, the Soviet Union and the United States.

Many of the most important issues that the world confronts demand international solutions. Let us begin with the maintenance of peace. Arms control and disarmament are goals that can only become effective if there is international agreement about them. The existence of weapons of instantaneous mass destruction underlines the indispensability of such international agreement and also demands a network of immediate unambiguous communication between the major nuclear powers. The 'hot line' between Washington and Moscow and those between other capitals are elements in this necessary network. So are the summit meetings among the major military and economic powers that are held intermittently. The establishment of understanding and if possible of trust between the world's rulers is the cement that holds the structure of peace together.

There are less dramatic threats to the survival of the human race than nuclear weapons, and these less dramatic threats also demand an international response. The pollution of the environment, the air, the seas and the great rivers, cannot be controlled by a single nation, however strong. The efforts of any one government can be nullified by the slackness of another. As for the destruction of the planet's irreplaceable natural resources of forests, fossil fuel and cultivable land, it is only too obvious that everyone's problem has been nobody's problem. Only very recently have the United Nations and other international bodies begun to preach the gospel of conservation, often to deaf ears in the governments of member states.

Interdependence in the economic field has grown with the enormous increase in world trade and the establishment of many multinational corporations. Little international trade is now conducted between metropolitan powers and their colonial dependencies, for the obvious reason that the imperial pattern of trade has been destroyed along with the empires themselves. But what many people fail to realize is that the post-imperial legacy of a familiar trade between Commonwealth countries is disappearing too. Britain, nearly half of whose exports went to Commonwealth countries after the war, now exports only 14 per cent to them. Britain and France used to be able to impose their own commercial rules, such as Imperial Preference, on many of their trading partners, but they are no longer strong enough to do so. The context in which economic policy is formulated is established largely by international movements of energy and raw materials prices, and by interest rates. No Western European country can establish its own interest rates without reference to the rates set by the US Federal Reserve Bank. And the United States, with the world's most powerful economy, critically influences the prospects for expansion or recession in the world.

Despite their nominal independence, the countries of the Third World are constrained by their financial dependence on the major powers. They are buffeted by OPEC's decisions on oil prices and burdened by high interest rates on the huge debts they have incurred to pay for essential imports, especially of oil. These interest rates are established in the financial centres of the West, New York, Tokyo, London, Paris and Frankfurt, and it is the Western governments and Japan who dominate international economic institutions such as the International Monetary Fund and the World Bank. Countries in economic trouble, compelled to borrow from rich countries or from the international institutions, are required to conform to orthodox economic and financial policies – as British governments know very well.

There is no escape from interdependence in the Soviet bloc either. The East European countries and such dependent allies as Cuba are constrained to buy their raw materials and oil from the Soviet Union at prices she establishes, and to pay for them with exports often sold for less than they would get in world markets. The Soviet Union has not been able to meet the capital demands of her allies; hence they, and indeed the Soviet Union herself, have raised substantial sums of investment capital in the West, and owe large debts especially to the Federal Republic of Germany. The division between the ideological blocs has been bridged by their mutual economic and financial requirements.

THE SHORT-SIGHTED RICH

Political institutions do not reflect this growing interdependence. United Nations actions are still subject to veto by the great powers of the Second World War. Attempts to establish peacekeeping forces have been one-sided owing to the non-involvement of the Soviet bloc, and are anyway only operative in situations where every significant nation agrees to their use. None of the international economic institutions include the Soviet Union, and all are effectively controlled by the United States and her main European allies. Third World pleas for a new international economic order, in which the rich countries would support the prices of primary products, and link the prices of their own manufactured exports to the prices of the main Third World exports, have not got very far. The inadequacy of our international institutions was most strikingly illustrated by the absence of any international political initiative to deal with the oil crisis.

The developing countries who are not producers of oil face colossally increased energy bills and high interest rates which together may break their frail economic and political systems. The oil deficit for the Third World was estimated for 1980 alone at between $65,000 and $70,000 million,[1] plus half as much again in interest on rising debts. The world banking system has recycled part of the oil surpluses, some of them into investment in Third World countries; but without substantial additional lending on favourable terms by the International Monetary Fund, the World Bank and other inter-governmental institutions, large deficits will continue to overshadow the world's markets. Developing countries will attempt to reduce their deficits by cutting back on imports, and such attempts will in turn depress production in the industrial countries.

The scale of the crisis demands a political initiative that has not been forthcoming. At the Western economic summit in Venice in June 1980 the major Western countries turned away from the Third World challenge, clearly set out though it was by the Brandt Commission, and devoted themselves instead to attacking inflation within the developed countries of the West, pursuing orthodox financial policies incompatible with any attempt to rescue the Third World. Squeezing out inflation in the West unmodified by any policy to create effective demand in the Third World looks like a recipe for worsening the international recession. Western leaders, unable to see any problems but their own, remind one of Machiavelli's aphorism, 'In the country of the blind, the one-eyed man is king.'

In the earlier chapters of this book, I argued that governments, together with the great corporate powers of industry and the trade unions, should devolve some of their powers downwards, and should encourage greater participation through industrial democracy, tenant management of housing and in other ways. But governments also have to concede some of their powers to international institutions if there is to be peace and reasonable prosperity in the world. The inadequacy of our international institutions, who wield power over the weak in the name of the strong, has led to disappointment and frustration. That disappointment and frustration can lead countries to reject their international role. After the First World War, the United States, frustrated by the shortsighted and cynical policies of its European allies, entered a long period of isolationism. Had it not done so there might not have been a Second World War. France, under de Gaulle, pulled out of NATO's command structure in 1966, and attempted to pursue her own political and military strategies with only very limited success. Now Britain is being urged towards economic isolationism by voices on the left and on the far right of politics. She is being urged to withdraw from the European Community and adopt a protectionist trade policy.

Britain is one of the least likely countries to be able to make a success of a siege economy. She is dependent on the rest of the world for almost half her food and two thirds of her raw materials. One in three jobs is connected with overseas trade. Of that trade over 43 per cent is now done with the European Community, seven of whose member-states now figure among Britain's ten best export markets. The European Community now acts as negotiator for all its members in trade negotiations, for instance in the Tokyo round of the GATT, and in reaching commercial agreements with India, China and other countries. No single European country on its own could possibly negotiate equivalent terms, nor prevent retaliation against protectionist measures. Those who believe that Britain could raise general tariff barriers against imports of manufactures without risk of retaliation should look at her payments balances. Why should countries like the United States, with a serious payments deficit, accept increased tariffs against American imports from a country with a healthy payments surplus, albeit derived from North Sea oil? Even selective controls or steps to prevent dumping need to be backed by effective economic power, a power Britain on her own does not possess.

THE EUROPEAN COMMUNITY: OPTING OUT

In an interdependent world countries cannot opt out, however much they might want to do so, without causing great damage to themselves. The damage to Britain caused by withdrawal from the European Community would be so extensive as practically to rule it out of practical politics. Quite apart from the damage to British trade there would be a virtual cessation of international investment in Britain, which has been the main beneficiary of American investment in the European Community since our original entry in 1973.

The damage would not be limited to British relations with the rest of the Community, however. Britain's significance to her other friends and allies would seriously diminish. The United States and the Commonwealth countries see Britain as a friend influencing the Community in their favour. India, Nigeria and, most recently, Zimbabwe have used their Commonwealth associations with Britain to try to get trading preferences or investment or aid from the Community. Not a single Commonwealth country has urged British withdrawal. Indeed almost all of them lobbied vigorously at the time of the 1975 referendum for Britain to stay in. A British withdrawal would be a bitter blow to developing Commonwealth countries, and would weaken our ties with them. Those who advocate the withdrawal of Britain from the European Community usually advance two arguments. The first is that Britain's economic position has been weakened by membership and that, in particular, Britain's trade balance has suffered severely. The second is that the Common Agricultural Policy is expensive, inefficient and particularly burdensome for Britain.

The first objection is not borne out by what has happened since 1973. Both exports and imports between Britain and her Community partners have grown much faster than between Britain and the rest of the world, exports more than twice as fast. The stimulus to exports promised by advocates of British entry into the European Community has in fact occurred; the British share of world trade fell by 11.9 per cent between 1951 and 1972, an average of 0.6 per cent a year; between 1972 and 1979, it declined only 0.3 per cent in all. In those same seven years total British exports to the European Community increased by an average of 16.8 per cent a year, measured in Deutschmarks. Total imports from the European Community rose by an average of 16.4 per cent a year.[2] British exports in the first nine months of 1980 paid for 97 per cent of imports from the Community, compared to 70 per cent at the time of the referendum.[3] The National Institute's *Review* for November 1978 declared: 'U K–E E C trade has grown faster than might have been expected in the absence of entry, with little or no loss of non-agricultural trade in other markets.'[4]

It is true that British exports of manufactures to the Community have been less successful than British exports of other goods. Indeed, the trade deficit on manufacturing goods rose from £556m in 1975 to £2,731m in 1979, a substantial increase in real terms. However, those who favour withdrawal rarely point out that the ratio of manufacturing exports to manufacturing imports with the rest of the world has deteriorated much more rapidly than with the European Community. The weakness of the manufacturing sector in Britain is not a consequence of membership of the Community; it is a consequence of Britain's declining competitivity in making cars, even for the home market, and in particular of the appalling record of one huge corporation, British Leyland. The serious imbalance in trade in cars is responsible for most of the deterioration in Britain's manufacturing trade balance.

The second objection is based on stronger grounds. The Common Agricultural Policy, in effect the price Germany paid to France for a common market in industrial goods, is ill-adapted for Britain's agricultural structure of fairly large farms employing very few people. The system of financing the Common Agricultural Policy partly by levies on imports of agricultural produce is also unfavourable to Britain, much the largest importer of non-Community foodstuffs. The Common Agricultural funds account for three quarters of the Community's budget; their size and the method of financing them have seriously distorted Community net budgetary contributions to Britain's disadvantage. In 1980, Britain, the third poorest country in the European Community, found herself expected to contribute a net £800 millions to the Community budget, enough to make her the largest contributor of all.

An interim solution limiting Britain's contribution for the next three years was agreed in the autumn of 1980, owing to the willingness of the German government to increase its own payments to the Community. In the longer term, a major reconstruction of the Common Agricultural Policy is inescapable.

THE COMMON AGRICULTURAL POLICY

The Europe of the Nine, to which Greece has now been added, is shortly to become the Europe of the Twelve. That further expansion will require a new approach to the Common Agricultural Policy, because it will be impossible to finance agriculture in an expanded Community on the present basis. Indeed, the crisis will come even sooner for the CAP, for its budget will soon break through the ceiling set by 'own resources' (a combination of import levies and a 1 per cent share of value added tax) at a time when few member governments will be inclined to increase them. The Community's agricultural policy cannot simply be abolished. It is the most significant common structure the Community has. It suffers, however, from distortions which are impossible to justify, and which are becoming more serious. The Community's agricultural funds are divided into two, a guarantee fund under which prices of most agricultural products are maintained by the commitment that, if prices fall below a fixed intervention price, the Community will purchase the residue; and a structural fund to finance modernization, bigger and more viable farms (many continental farms are under 20 hectares, British farms being on average two or three times bigger), and the transfer of people out of farming. Unfortunately the guarantee fund has swamped the structural fund, which now commands less than 5 per cent of the Community's overall agricultural budget.

Within the guarantee fund, support is not linked to farm income but to output. In other words, the larger a farm's output the more it benefits from the Community's guarantee funds. There is a good egalitarian argument for maintaining the incomes of small farmers, either as a transitional measure or as a permanent social policy; but there is no argument for making rich farmers even richer out of the pockets of consumers as the Common Agricultural Policy does – a clear case of regressive taxation.

The Common Agricultural Policy is regressive in another way as well. A much larger proportion of the guarantee fund goes to traditional northern European agricultural products such as beef, wheat, milk and butter, over two fifths to the dairy sector alone, than to the products of the poorer Mediterranean regions, such as olive oil, horticultural products and rice. This imbalance cannot survive the accession of Spain, Portugal and Greece. Britain would have allies not least among socialists in the continental member countries in supporting a greater emphasis on the structural fund, a fairer distribution of guarantees across the product range, and above all a link between price guarantees and income maintenance for farmers, so that guarantees would be gradually phased out for those whose income exceeded a reasonable level.

The expansion of the Community could lead to a recasting of the Common Agricultural Policy based on transitional support for Europe's small farmers and peasants until agriculture helped by the structural fund has achieved a reasonable level of competitiveness. For socialists it is not an ignoble purpose, since small farmers represent the least prosperous occupational group in the extended Community.

EUROPEAN OPPORTUNITY

The Common Agricultural Policy in its present form has soured the attitude of the British public to the European Community, but it is not the only reason why Britain has been at best a reluctant partner in the Community and at worst a hostile one. Historically, Britain has remained isolated from the Continent, involving herself only when the balance of power was threatened by the domination of one European nation over it. The Channel has made the course of the island's history significantly different from that of the Continent; neither invasion nor occupation has overtaken Britain for a thousand years, since a national administration was established by the Normans. It is therefore easy for Britain to underestimate the greatest achievement of the Community's creators, which was to make another war between Western European countries unthinkable. Furthermore, the timing of Britain's entry into the Community could hardly have been more unfortunate. As Willy Brandt has pointed out, Britain joined in the very year, 1973, that Western economic prospects began to darken. The Community has been held responsible for rising inflation, deepening recession and the other economic discontents of these past seven years, often quite unjustly. Certainly the Common Agricultural Policy contributed to higher food prices, but its contribution was much less significant than other factors, such as increased energy costs. Between 1973 and 1980 the CAP added about 19 per cent to food prices, which rose by nearly 200 per cent overall.

There is another reason, however, and it is an ironic one. Britain seems to have deliberately made the least possible use of the opportunities offered to her by the Community. The British citizen receives only half as much Community spending per head as the average Community citizen. This was due partly to a lack of knowledge, now largely rectified, among local authorities and others about the opportunities available, partly to the British government's unwillingness to stump up its share of social and regional expenditure. Community funds cannot be substituted for national government expenditure; they must be additional. Often they are counterpart funds, matching the national government's contribution. This makes it all the more regrettable that the British government has on occasion been unwilling to offer its share. Community money is available for industrial training, for job creation, for community enterprise, for moving families to where jobs are, and for tiding over people made redundant in the coal and steel industries by maintaining their incomes. Britain has consistently taken less advantage of such funds than other Community countries.

Nor has Britain shown much interest in reforms that might have been expected to attract the attention of socialists, if not of Conservatives – for example the fifth directive on industrial democracy, which requires that workpeople be represented on the boards of large companies or the code of conduct for multinational companies. The Commission has pressed for equal pay and equal working conditions for men and women, another cause that might have been expected to attract the support of radicals. Under the Lomé convention, which includes the associated countries in Africa and the Caribbean, the Community has undertaken to stabilize the incomes of primary producers. General preferences on a wide range of imported products have been agreed with major Third World countries like India. The Community and its member-states are now much more significant sources of aid to developing countries than either the United States or the Soviet Union. Socialists might be expected to support all these policies, and most socialist members of the European Parliament do so. But the British ones get little encouragement from Westminster or from the Labour party.

The European Community, being an institution, is a vehicle for ideas and policies. It is not itself an ideology, though those who created it dreamed of a European federation. Within the context of Europe itself, the Community can have a conservative or a socialist flavour and can be more or less internationalist. The Community has much more weight in international negotiations on commerce and trade than any of its individual members, and it could have considerable political weight as well. The first tentative steps have been taken to establish a dialogue with the Arab states and even with the Palestine Liberation Organization to explore the chances of a lasting and peaceful settlement in the Middle East. This is a new departure, for generally the Community has resisted taking any significant political role. Germany is still reluctant to accept the political leadership her economic strength could ensure her. France and Britain are absorbed in proving to themselves that they are still great powers, morally if not economically, and therefore they seek to act on their own. Gradually, however, in the United Nations and elsewhere, the Community is beginning to adopt a common posture. As the 1979 report of the Council of Foreign Ministers put it, 'The Europe of the Nine is increasingly regarded by the external world as a coherent entity in world affairs.'

If the Community began to realize the potential inherent in being a 'coherent entity' in world affairs, it could alter the forbidding prospects the world now faces. I have written earlier about the need for a new initiative on recycling the oil surpluses and on creating effective demand in the Third World to counter the world recession. The Community could not bring about such a transformation of the economic outlook on its own, but it could propose a plan based on the conclusions of the Brandt Commission, and try to involve the superpowers too. Such a plan might embody a radical new idea to which the Brandt Report refers, the idea that a small percentage of each country's gross national product, perhaps 1 per cent or even less, should be earmarked for multilateral aid to the Third World. Because the new tax would be linked to gross national product, it would be progressive as between countries. It would be a first step away from the concept of charity towards the concept of social justice – a first step that Western European countries took for themselves early in this century when alms from the rich were replaced by the elements of a welfare state financed in part from taxation. Until that step is taken, there will be neither a guarantee of continuity of funds nor a structure of redistribution of wealth on however modest a scale between nations as there is within nations. No single European country, with the possible exception of

Germany, could hope to get any such scheme off the ground – but the Community could.

DÉTENTE AND DISARMAMENT

The European Community could also become a force for disarmament, and one that must seek peace, for in any major nuclear war its destruction would be certain. Individual European countries have attempted unilateral initiatives to ease tensions or to end regional wars, but the record has been inauspicious. The Labour governments of 1964 to 1970 made a series of ineffective attempts to end the Vietnam War, which got nowhere despite Britain's supposed 'special relationship' with the United States. President Giscard d'Estaing has pursued isolated initiatives in the Middle East and Africa, and tried in 1980 to engage in a bilateral dialogue with the Soviet Union on matters of international concern, without raising much enthusiasm there. The only significant recent initiative towards peace that seriously interested the Soviet Union was the visit by Helmut Schmidt, speaking on behalf of the Community, to Moscow in June 1980, which led to an agreement with President Brezhnev to discuss the possibility of a mutual withdrawal · of medium-range nuclear weapons from Europe. The Federal Republic has worked hard to get détente in central Europe, and managed to achieve a big increase in trade across the border and the reunification of German families by thousands of visits from West Germany to East Germany. Until the Soviet invasion of Afghanistan and the strikes in Poland, Germany's *Ostpolitik* had been notably successful in easing tension along the border between the Soviet bloc and the NATO bloc. But the *Ostpolitik* would not have been possible without the Federal Republic's membership of the European Community. Any rapprochement with the German Democratic Republic would have aroused intense suspicion in Western Europe, Soviet Russia and the United States that the two German states were seeking to re-unite. Nor would the *Ostpolitik* have been possible in internal political terms had the Federal Republic not been a member of the EEC, for the Christian Democrats would have cast doubt on the Socialist government's commitment to Western democracy.

The Community has already made détente in Europe possible. It can now contribute to a wider détente between the superpowers. The Community is the only political entity in the world strong enough to make the superpowers take multilateral disarmament seriously at a time when neither, for internal political reasons, is inclined to do so. A framework for multilateral disarmament negotiations is a *sine qua non* of world peace, and the European Community has an excellent opportunity to begin erecting such a framework through negotiations on European theatre nuclear weapons following Chancellor Schmidt's initiative. The Soviet Union is clearly disturbed about the prospect of Cruise missiles being installed in Western Europe. A considerable barrage of propaganda has been directed at the governments of Belgium, the Netherlands, Italy, Germany and Britain to persuade them not to accept delivery of Cruise missiles. Meanwhile the Soviet Union has continued to install medium-range nuclear missiles, the SS 20s, in Eastern Europe and western Russia at a fairly rapid rate. European Community countries are in a strong position to press for mutual withdrawal of these weapons.

Whatever the claims made for unilateral disarmament, it is highly unlikely that either the Soviet Union or the United States would follow the example of a Holland or a Britain that had surrendered all nuclear weapons. After all, the superpowers have shown no signs of following the examples of Japan and Austria, both of whom have abided by the repudiation of nuclear weapons written into their peace treaties. One argument for unilateral nuclear disarmament is that it would make the disarmed country a safer place, less likely to be attacked. Whatever the merits of that argument, it is surely clear that means would still need to be found to influence the superpowers towards peace, since any strategic nuclear exchange between them would cause great damage and destruction throughout the world, including those countries that had abandoned nuclear weapons. That is why the development of the European Community's political role in seeking détente in Europe and in pursuing arms limitation is more important for world peace than unilateral nuclear disarmament in one or a few countries can ever be. There are strong moral arguments for refusing to use nuclear weapons against any other country. But they should not be confused with the unconvincing political argument that such a refusal would make a country safe from nuclear destruction. Unilateral nuclear disarmament cannot be a substitute for creating effective political institutions to control arms and to prevent war. It is in building up and strengthening such institutions that the Community could be crucial, as it could be crucial for a new deal for the developing world.

The next few years will bring about important internal changes in the European Community. Britain has an opportunity that will not recur to influence those changes so that the Community becomes more flexible and more responsive to the social needs of the people within it, as well as to the world outside. The Community is entering a period in which international tensions could be heightened by a right-wing American President surrounded by advisers who believe in a strong military posture and by the strains of deciding upon a successor to Mr Brezhnev in the Soviet Union at a time of turbulence in Eastern Europe. The Community is going to be badly needed as a force for peace and stability. For Britain to contemplate changes in it is sensible and changes are bound to come. But for Britain to withdraw would be to abdicate from responsibility at a dangerous time for the world.

14

Conclusion: Politics is for People

Power corrupts, said Lord Acton. Yet most men and women who join political parties or who embark upon a political career do so with the intention of bettering the lives of their fellow human beings. Politics is not a dishonourable calling. In order to bring about the improvements they seek, politicians must acquire power. The temptation of politics is to seek power for itself and for the status it confers. At that point the original purpose for which power was acquired is lost or forgotten.

If politics is to be for people, then the first requirement is that the powers of government must be limited, that those in power must be accountable to the people, and that governments must be able to be changed if they forfeit popular support. Socialism without liberty is not worth having, for socialism without liberty will in time create a new and arrogant ruling class.

To enhance our liberty, information should not be restricted by the executive, unless it affects national security. In Britain, a freedom of information Act is overdue. It should be complemented by legislation to prevent unauthorized use of information about individuals. Computerization and microelectronics could threaten the privacy and ultimately the freedom of individuals unless safeguards are built into the system of official record keeping. Sweden has a permanent watchdog committee to ensure that such safeguards are maintained.

The imbalance of power between the legislature and the executive in Britain is gradually being corrected in favour of the legislature by the activities of the new Select Committees. In future, new legislation should be submitted to them in draft, before it is presented as a Bill to Parliament. If a major change is proposed, a consultative paper should be published and debated in Parliament before legislation is drafted. In these ways Parliament could ensure the element of continuity so badly needed in Britain's jerky and mutually antipathetic succession of governments.

Central government is the pinnacle of a self-governing society, but it is only part of the governing process. So other reforms are needed to strengthen the structure of self-government at lower levels too. This is crucial if power is to be diffused throughout society and if ordinary people are to be given greater control over their own lives. Industrial democracy should be required by law, but there should be an option between a consultative committee at every level or worker representation on the company's board. If politics is for people, then workers must have the right to choose their representatives, though constituencies could be created to reflect various occupational groups. School governing bodies, hospital administration and the management of housing estates all lend themselves to participation by those affected. So do the social services, through mutual help, family grouping and the use of volunteers, especially people who have experienced and overcome the disabilities faced by those in need. If the welfare state is for people, then people must not be reduced to being seen as claimants or clients. Poverty is in the person as well as in the purse; its abolition demands the restoration of a human being's self-respect and dignity as well as meeting his or her material needs. The same is true of the treatment of elderly, ill or dying people. Sophisticated medical techniques may be part of the treatment, but they are less important to a person's peace of mind and happiness than individual care. Britain has found a humane answer to caring for elderly people in purpose-built bungalows and self-contained flats linked to common social and catering facilities and to a warden on twenty-four-hour call. Equally humane ways of caring for chronically sick or mentally handicapped people remain to be found; mutual help through artificial family groups may be one way.

Emphasis on the quality of people's lives suggests new ways of organizing industry, ways that will be encouraged by microelectronics. Industry will be able to be more decentralized; a lot of work will be done from home, or organized to suit individual timetables. Innovative small firms should flourish, given a fair wind by central and local government and adequate venture capital from public agencies and the banks. The danger, however, is that the decentralization of work could leave the old inner cities as abandoned deserts of unemployment and poverty. So the advent of the new technologies must be coupled with a fresh attack on poverty and on unemployment.

A national traineeship scheme for all school-leavers, complemented by access to advanced education for those with vocational qualifications as well as those with academic qualifications, would greatly improve young people's chances of getting a job. Some of those jobs could be created by a policy of conserving energy and raw materials though insulating the housing stock and recycling used materials. More radically, public policies should be reviewed to remove disincentives to the use of labour compared to other factors of production. Many of our institutions are subtly shaped to discourage the employment of people, as compared to capital or land or raw materials. One reason for this is that people in large numbers are difficult to manage; if there were fewer large plants there might actually be more jobs.

STEADY GROWTH

A modest steady growth rate could be attained in the industrialized countries providing that inflationary pressures could be restrained and providing also that there was sufficient demand. On the former, I have argued that inflationary pressures are partly produced by corporate power – centralized industrial and labour markets – and that a decentralization of power would weaken those pressures. That will take time; in the short run, an incomes policy is needed, and I have attempted to show how it might work. A national campaign to explain the need for an incomes policy is essential, as is a broadening of bargaining aims so that wage increases are not the sole measure of bargaining success.

Britain's economic weakness is most marked in manufacturing and, within manufacturing, in two industries, cars and textiles. There are other sources of concern, not least the mismatch between old skills and new technologies. But the country has a remarkable record of invention and innovation. It has fine broadcasting services, good software, excellent science, good though conservative universities; it still retains a strong civic sense and a remarkably uncorrupt civil service. If the political parties accepted the mixed economy as the pattern of the future and supported success in whichever sector it occurred, Britain's prospects would be transformed. The public sector would be free to borrow from commercial sources for wealth-creating activities and such borrowing would not be included within the public sector borrowing requirement. The National Enterprise Board would be able to retain its stake in successful private companies, using the return on its capital to finance new holdings elsewhere; it would be possible to launch new publicly owned companies to compete with private companies in sectors where profits are high or where the main purchasers are public authorities; pharmaceuticals is a good example. Public agencies would provide venture capital for new public sector enterprises like industrial cooperatives. A small business agency and local enterprise trusts jointly established by local authorities and industry would provide the expert advice and help many small enterprises need to get off the ground. Tax incentives would be directed rather towards investment for expansion than to investment for rationalization; new firms would be helped by a tax holiday. And if power is to be diffused, a much tougher policy towards monopolies and mergers would be needed, including within such a policy business practices that discourage small customers and small suppliers. Decentralization and participation are conducive to greater individual liberty and to fraternity because they restore to people their wholeness; they become, as I said in Chapter 1, members of society in all its aspects, instead of being merely economic instruments of the production process.

But decentralization and participation are not necessarily conducive to equality. The experience of countries where schools are governed by representatives of the local community, as in the United States, or where works councils are elected in every factory or plant, as in Germany, is that only a minority shows any real interest. That minority is more articulate and often better educated than the unconcerned majority. So a new division is created, between the participators and those they represent or even use. Furthermore, decentralized power makes it easier for rich regions or rich localities to maintain their advantages against poor regions or localities. The ratio between the resources spent on a child in the poorest school districts of the decentralized federal US education system and the richest ones is of the order of six to one. In Britain, where education finances are funded as to 60 per cent from central government, the ratio is about 1.4 to one.

CLASS AND SEGREGATION

It is a difficult balance to get right. Redistribution of income and wealth through taxation, widened as I have suggested, must continue. Higher child benefit would help poor families whether the parents are in work or unemployed. A return to full employment would remove much potential poverty. For the very old, sheltered accommodation and friendship is at least as important as higher pensions. But at the heart of inequality are unequal opportunities and vast differences in life-styles. Both, at least in Britain, relate to class. So education and housing policies are central to the attack on inequality. I have advocated an integrated approach by the health and education services to pre-school children, so that the handicapped and disadvantaged can be positively helped. Vocational and academic courses should be combined in school and subsequently in tertiary and sixth-form colleges, and vocational qualifications should be recognized. Children should not be socially segregated; hence independent schools should be integrated within a system of maintained schools that offers parents a choice within the state system, of subjects, of coeducation or single-sex schools, of denominational or county schools, and even of schools with different approaches to rules and discipline.

Housing has been segregated as well as education, into council estates and private estates. Because most schools are neighbourhood schools, socially segregated housing becomes the foundation of socially segregated schools. A truly classless education system requires different housing policies. Providing there is an adequate stock of housing for rent, the sale of council houses helps to break down the segregated social structure. But sales of council houses should be associated with local authority infilling of sites and conversion of large old houses into flats for rent in areas of privately owned housing. The new popularity of rehabilitation may help to create a more varied pattern of residence; such a pattern could restore life to the inner cities, as is happening in parts of Glasgow and London, and also create more balanced communities in the big overspill estates constructed in the 1950s and 1960s.

A programme of radical reform in Britain or in any other country can only be achieved over a decade or more; but world time is running out faster than that. None of us dare become so absorbed in our internal problems that we neglect the dangers of the arms race or the desperation of the millions who are poor and hungry. If politics is for people, it is for these people too, whose cultures have been threatened by our technologies and whose resources have been plundered for our factories. The governments of the industrialized world could harness their own unemployed resources to the almost infinite needs of the Third World; the money to finance a new Marshall Plan could be found by diverting to it part of current arms expenditure, by using the payments surpluses of the oil producers and by a tax on gross national products as suggested in Chapter 13. Given the hope of prosperity, developing countries would begin to abandon their swords for ploughshares.

This is of course a vision, and as such will be rejected as not being practical politics. Practical politics is about ruling classes, bureaucrats, parties, lobbies, interests and advancement. It is about making people fit into the requirements of technological processes because technological processes increase the quantity of goods and services, whatever their effect for good or bad on the quality of human life. But the old politics is dying. The battle to decide what the new politics will be like is just beginning. It is possible, just possible, that it will be a politics for people.

Notes

I. THE ACHIEVEMENT

1. Beveridge, W., *Social Insurance and Allied Services: Report*, London, HMSO, November 1942.
2. Keynes, J. M., *The General Theory of Employment, Interest and Money*, London, Macmillan, 1936.
3. ibid.
4. Dahrendorf, Ralf, *Life Chances*, London, Weidenfeld & Nicolson, 1979.
5. Burns, A., 'The anguish of central banking', the 1979 Per Jacobsson Lecture given at the American Enterprise Institute, September 1979.
6. Kristol, Irving, in *Dialogue*, vol. 12, no. 3, 1979, p. 47.
7. Marx, Karl, *Criticism of the Gotha Programme*, 1875, after Bakunin.
8. Marx, Karl, *The Civil War in France*, 1871.
9. Crosland, C. A. R., *The Future of Socialism*, London, Cape, 1956.
10. Tawney, R. H., *The Attack and Other Papers*, London, Allen & Unwin, 1953.
11. Tawney, R. H., *Equality*, London, Allen & Unwin, 1931.
12. Williams, Philip, *Hugh Gaitskell*, London, Cape, 1979.
13. The Army Debates at Putney, 29 October 1647, quoted by Peacock, Edward, 'Life of Rainborowe', *Archaeologia*, xlvi, 48.

2. WHAT WENT WRONG

1. King, Anthony, 'Overload: problems of governing in the 1970s', *Political Studies*, vol. 23, June/September 1975.
2. According to the *Health and Personal Social Security Statistics* (London,

HMSO, 1978) the number of medical staff employed in the National Health Service and the personal social services in Great Britain rose from 783,030 in 1972 to 898,127 in 1977; the number of administrative and clerical employees rose from 83,708 to 113,757 in the same period. The ratio of the first to the second fell from 9.3 : 1 to 7.9 : 1.

3. Bentham, Jeremy, *Panopticon, or the Inspection House*, London, 1791.

4. Williams, op. cit.

5. Stalin, Joseph, *Foundations of Leninism*, 1924, 'The party', sec. 3, 'The party as the highest form of class organization of the proletariat'.

6. *Inequalities in Health* (the report of a DHSS Research Working Group, chairman Sir Douglas Black), London, HMSO, 1980.

7. Djilas, Milovan, *The New Class, an Analysis of the Communist System*, London, Allen & Unwin, 1966.

8. Solzhenitsyn, Alexander, *The Gulag Archipelago*, vol. 1, London, Collins and the Harvill Press, 1974.

9. Dahrendorf, op. cit.

10. Kant, Immanuel, 'Idee zu einer allgemeinen Geschichte in weltbürgerlicher Absicht', published posthumously in Kant's *Gesammelte Schriften*, Berlin, 1902.

3. THE CHALLENGERS

1. Owen, Robert, *Observations on the Effect of the Manufacturing System*, 1815.

2. Polanyi, Karl, *The Great Transformation*, New York, Rinehart, 1944.

3. Hirsch, Fred, *Social Limits to Growth*, London, Routledge, 1977.

4. Larkin, Philip, *High Windows*, London, Faber, 1974.

5. Dahrendorf, op. cit.

6. Friedman, Milton and Rose, *Free to Choose*, London, Secker & Warburg, 1980; Penguin Books, 1980.

7. Leknehman, Robert, contribution to 'Capitalism, socialism and democracy', a symposium in *Commentary*, vol. 65, no. 4, April 1978.

8. Pinder, John, 'Economic revival waits on new policies and political reform', paper for the Beijer Institute Symposium, Nobel Symposium no. 49, Stockholm, August 1980.

9. *North-South: a Programme for Survival* (the report of the Independent Commission on International Development Issues, chairman Willy Brandt), London, Pan, 1980.

10. Tawney, R. H., *The Acquisitive Society*, New York, Harcourt Brace, 1920.

4. HOW THE WORLD HAS CHANGED

1. *Energy: the Next Twenty Years* (a report sponsored by the Ford Foundation), Cambridge, Mass., Ballinger Publishing Co., 1979.
2. Schelling, Thomas C., and the Design Committee on Long Range Energy Policy, *Thinking Through the Energy Problem*, New York, Committee for Economic Development, March 1979.
3. US National Academy of Sciences, *Energy and Climate*, Washington DC, 1977.
4. Medvedev, Zhores, *Nuclear Disaster in the Urals*, London, Angus & Robertson, 1979.
5. *Leakage of Radioactive Liquor into the Ground, BNFL, Windscale*, London, Health and Safety Executive, July 1980.
6. Ward, Barbara, *Progress for a Small Planet*, London, Maurice Temple Smith, 1979; Penguin Books, 1979.
7. *Economic Outlook*, Paris, OECD, December 1980.

5. THE NEW TECHNOLOGIES

1. Central Policy Review Staff, *Social and Employment Implications of Microelectronics*, London, CPRS, November 1978.
2. Likierman, Andrew, 'The impact of microelectronics on employment', *London Business School Journal*, vol. 4, part 2, Autumn 1979.
3. Friedrichs, Gunter, 'Microelectronics – a new dimension of technological change and automation', paper for the Club of Rome conference on 'The Coming Decade of Danger and Opportunity', Berlin, October 1979.
4. ACARD, ABRC and the Royal Society, *Biotechnology* (report of a joint working party), London, HMSO, March 1980.

6. THE THREAT OF UNEMPLOYMENT

1. Jenkins, Clive, and Sherman, Barry, *The Collapse of Work*, London, Eyre Methuen, 1979.
2. *Employment Gazette* (Department of Employment), vol. 88, no. 11, November 1980.
3. *Economic Outlook*, Paris, OECD, December 1980.
4. *Review of Youth Employment Policies in the United States*, Paris, OECD, August 1980.

5. Manpower Services Commission, *Review of the Second Year of Special Programmes*, July 1980.
6. ibid.

7. A POLICY FOR FULL EMPLOYMENT

1. White, Michael, *Shorter Working Time*, London, Policy Studies Institute, December 1980.
2. *Employment Gazette* (Department of Employment), vol. 88, no. 11, November 1980.
3. Polanyi, op. cit.
4. Shonfield, Andrew, *The Attack on World Poverty*, London, Chatto & Windus, 1960.
5. Lutz, Meriaux, Mukhterjee and Rehn, *Outlook for Employment in the European Community to 1980*, Brussels, Commission of the European Communities, July 1976.
6. Giles, W. J., and Robinson, D. F., *Human Asset Accounting*, London, Institute of Personnel Management and the Institute of Cost and Management Accountants, 1972.
7. Likert, Rensis, *The Human Organization: its Management and Value*, New York, McGraw Hill, 1967, quoted in Giles and Robinson, op. cit.
8. Giles and Robinson, op. cit.
9. Law 79/10, Création des Enterprises par les Chômeurs, 3 January 1979.

8. LESS CONCENTRATION: INDUSTRY

1. Eltis, Walter, 'How much is going wrong?', unpublished paper, April 1980.
2. Morgan, Ann, 'The balance of payments and British membership of the EEC', in Wallace, William, ed., *Britain in Europe*, London, Heinemann, 1980. The figures exclude erratic items like diamonds.
3. *National Institute Economic Review*, August 1980.
4. United Nations and OECD sources, quoted in 'German outlook: slightly cloudy with showers', *Vision*, June 1980.
5. Dunning, John H., *United States Industry in Britain*, London, Wilton House, 1976.
6. Policy Studies Institute, *Microprocessors: an Interim Report on Applications in Manufacturing*, London, PSI, December 1979.

7. National statistical censuses, quoted in 'Small and medium sized firms in OECD countries', unpublished working paper 51.961, OECD, 1980.

8. Freeman, Christopher, ed., *The Role of Small Firms in Innovation in the United Kingdom since 1945* (report to the Bolton Committee), London, HMSO, 1971.

9. Abernathy, W., and Utterback, J. M., *Innovation and the Evolution of Technology in the Firm*, Cambridge, Mass., Harvard Business School, June 1976.

10. Unpublished paper, Massachusetts Institute of Technology Development Foundation, 1976.

11. Prakke, F., 'The management of the R and D interface', PhD thesis, Massachusetts Institute of Technology, 1974.

12. Gillman Research Associates Inc., *Indicators of International Trends in Technological Innovation*, US National Science Board, 1976, Appendix D.

13. 'OECD programme on small and medium sized firms', unpublished working paper, Directorate of Science, Technology and Industry, Paris, OECD.

14. *Vision*, June 1980, op. cit.

15. *A Review of Monopolies and Mergers Policy*, Cmnd 7198, London, HMSO, May 1978.

16. Advisory Council for Applied Research and Development, *R and D for Public Purchasing*, London, HMSO, February 1980.

17. *Vision*, June 1980, op. cit.

18. Prais, S. J., *The Evolution of Giant Firms in Britain*, Cambridge University Press, 1976.

19. *A Review of Monopolies and Mergers Policy*, op. cit.

20. *Vision*, May 1980.

21. *Report of the Committee to Review the Functioning of Financial Institutions* (chairman Sir Harold Wilson), Cmnd 7937, London, HMSO, June 1980.

22. Galbraith, J. K., 'The need for flexible policies', a talk broadcast by the South European Service of the BBC, 1980.

23. Policy Studies Institute, *Microprocessors*, op. cit.

24. Harvard Business School, working papers on the Japanese economy.

25. The 28th Stevenson Memorial Lecture, given at Chatham House, 29 November 1979; reprinted in *International Affairs*, vol. 56, January 1980.

9. MORE PARTICIPATION: TRADE UNIONS

1. Sharpf, Fritz, *Capitalism of Yesteryear – and of Tomorrow?*, Berlin, International Institute of Management, November 1979.

2. ibid.

3. Parker, Peter, 'Industry and democracy: is the corporate state inevitable?', the Rita Hinden Memorial Lecture, February 1979.

4. Peter Jenkins in the *Guardian*, 26 January 1979.

5. Examples are given in *Industrial Relations Review and Report*, July 1980.

10. SOCIAL SERVICES: INVOLVING PEOPLE

1. Commission of the European Community, *The Perception of Poverty in Europe*, Brussels, 1977.

2. Klein, Rudolf, *Social Policy in the Eighties*, Paris, OECD, forthcoming.

11. EDUCATION: GOOD SCHOOLS AND BAD CLASSES

1. Steadman, Jane, *Progress in Secondary Schools, Findings from the National Child Development Study*, London, National Children's Bureau, July 1980.

2. Jencks, Christopher, and others, *Inequality: a Re-assessment of the Effect of Family and Schooling in America*, New York, Basic Books, 1972; Penguin Books, 1975.

3. Coleman, James, *The Equality of Educational Opportunity*, Washington DC, US Government Printing Office, 1966.

4. Graham, P., *Whither Equality of Educational Opportunity?*, paper for the Institute of Educational Policy Studies, Harvard Graduate School of Education, February 1980.

5. Rutter, Michael, and others, *Fifteen Thousand Hours: Secondary Schools and their Effect on Children*, Somerset, Open Books Publishing, 1979.

6. *Changes in Mathematical Achievement 1973–78*, Denver, Co., National Assessment of Educational Progress, Education Commission of the States, 1979.

12. POLITICAL INSTITUTIONS

1. Kuhn, Thomas S., *The Structure of Scientific Revolutions* (International Encyclopedia of Unified Science), Phoenix, University of Chicago Press, 1962; 2nd ed., 1970.

2. ibid., p. 92.

3. Marsh, A., *Protest and Political Consciousness*, London, Sage Publications, 1977.

13. THE THIRD WORLD AND EUROPE:
CHALLENGE AND RESPONSE

1. 'Where are the borrowers', *Economist*, 1–7 November 1980. OPEC countries were estimated to have 115 billion dollars surplus in 1980 alone.

2. Eltis, op. cit.

3. Tugendhat, Christopher, 'The Common Market: an opportunity ignored?', lecture to the Institute of Directors' Conference, November 1980.

4. Daly, A. E., *National Institute of Economic and Social Research Review*, November 1978.

Index

Index

MORE ABOUT PENGUINS
AND PELICANS

For further information about books available from Penguins please write to Dept EP, Penguin Books Ltd, Harmondsworth, Middlesex UB7 0DA.

In the U.S.A.: For a complete list of books available from Penguins in the United States write to Dept CS, Penguin Books, 625 Madison Avenue, New York, New York 10022.

In Canada: For a complete list of books available from Penguins in Canada write to Penguin Books Canada Ltd, 2801 John Street, Markham, Ontario L3R 1B4.

In Australia: For a complete list of books available from Penguins in Australia write to the Marketing Department, Penguin Books, Australia Ltd, P.O. Box 257, Ringwood, Victoria 3134.

In New Zealand: For a complete list of books available from Penguins in New Zealand write to the Marketing Department, Penguin Books (NZ) Ltd, P.O. Box 4019, Auckland 10.

A Penguin Special

PROTEST AND SURVIVE

Edited by E. P. Thompson and Dan Smith

Have cruise missiles increased the chances of nuclear war?

Nukes are nasty and governments are anxious to ensure that nuclear wars are 'limited' to a 'theatre'. Cruise missiles deployed in the UK are seen by the British government as preserving our ancient independence in the face of the 'monstrous' Russian threat.

In this book E. P. Thompson and his colleagues challenge the grounds of this assumption and show that use of the owner-controlled missiles by the US in a 'limited' war will mean the complete destruction of the 'theatre', of Western Europe and of Great Britain in particular.

So, how likely is it? Cruise missiles which enable attack deep within the Soviet Union will at least allow the US to fight on our soil rather than on theirs. That, combined with the belligerent beliefs of many western governments, the paranoia of Russia and the bureaucratization of mass destruction, turns what used to be a remote possibility into a frightening probability.

This book examines the politics of what is being done and, in the face of the British government's extraordinary pamphlet *Protect and Survive*, urges immediate and determined opposition.

ARGUMENTS FOR SOCIALISM

Tony Benn

The most controversial figure in British politics, Tony Benn outlines a strong democratic-socialist approach to the most crucial issues in our political life over the next decade.

'Benn's faith in the capacity of ordinary people to govern themselves emerges here as the most attractive feature of the politics of a man so often caricatured by the popular press as the Labour Party's major threat to democracy and freedom' – David Coats in the *Literary Review*

'Of importance not only to the Labour movement but also to the country as a whole' – Giles Radice in the *Tribune*

'Lively and provocative' – Paul Johnson in the *Sunday Telegraph*

THE LEFT IN BRITAIN 1956–1968

David Widgery

In Hungary in 1956 Stalin's tanks blew apart the Left in the rest of the world. Old complacencies were shattered, while new parties, new ideas and events brought a new militancy. The ferment continued for a decade and burst out in 1968 in Paris and across much of the world.

This book tells the story of those years in Britain, The New Left, CND, student politics, civil rights and a transformed trade union movement can all be seen springing up from that initial catastrophic break-up. David Widgery has written a lucid and exciting narrative of a time when the Left seemed invincible on the streets and impotent everywhere else. Each of his chapters is extensively illustrated by documents, pamphlets and articles showing how working-class movements combined with middle-class writers to bring about a completely changed understanding of what it now means to be 'on the Left'.

Inside politics and current events in Pelicans

WILL THE SOVIET UNION SURVIVE UNTIL 1984?

Andrei Amalrik

First published in 1970, Amalrik's essay was hailed by the *Guardian* as 'a brave unique voice from the Soviet Union coolly and pessimistically explaining the reality of that society and (a little less coolly) outlining his vision of the apocalypse to come, with the rise of China and the revival of nationalism among the non-Russian Soviet peoples'; while the *Sunday Times* called it 'literally the first piece of serious political analysis, based on experience, observation and undogmatic deduction, to have emerged from Russia for fifty years'.

In 1976 Amalrik left the Soviet Union. His original essay is reprinted here, as immediate and pertinent as ever, accompanied by a selection of Amalrik's major recent statements, written both in the Soviet Union and in exile.

WHO'S WATCHING YOU?

BRITAIN'S SECURITY SERVICES AND THE OFFICIAL SECRETS ACT

Crispin Aubrey

A probing account of the British security system.

The security services, invisible, unaccountable, surrounded by a mystique of dark glasses and turned-up collars, have grown steadily in size; so too has their expenditure on the most sophisticated techniques of mass surveillance.

Their net falls on trade unionists, students, anti-nuclear protesters, Welsh Nationalists, investigative journalists and a host of possible 'subversives'; Crispin Aubrey stumbled into this web one dark and rainy night in 1977, was arrested by the Special Branch and charged under the Official Secrets Act. His subsequent trial, the 'ABC trial', attained a legal significance and had political repercussions far beyond the facts of the case.

BEATING THE TERRORISTS?

INTERROGATION IN OMAGH, GOUGH AND CASTLEREAGH

Peter Taylor

Internationally condemned for ill-treating prisoners in 1971, Britain stands accused once again.

Why was the ill-treatment not stopped? Was it a systematic instrument of policy sanctioned from above?

Using dramatic new evidence, this book documents the inside story of interrogation by the Royal Ulster Constabulary from 1976–9 and the accompanying political cover-up.

A PLACE APART

Dervla Murphy

'An extraordinarily successful attempt to present Northern Ireland from the inside out, with honesty, sympathy and understanding' – *The Times Literary Supplement*

Unfettered by sectarian attitudes and armed with a delighted curiosity, Dervla Murphy cycled from the south into the mayhem of Northern Ireland and travelled extensively through both town and country. Frequently she found herself in horrifying situations, and sometimes among people stiff with hate and grief; but, equally, she discovered an unquenchable spirit everywhere that refuses to die.

Penguins on women's issues

DUTIFUL DAUGHTERS
WOMEN TALK ABOUT THEIR LIVES
Edited by Jean McCrindle and Sheila Rowbotham

'As remarkable and immediate as Oscar Lewis's *Children of Sanchez* ... an extraordinary compilation of the voices and memoirs of women over the past half century' – Emma Tennant in the *Guardian*.

THE WISE WOUND
MENSTRUATION & EVERYWOMAN
Penelope Shuttle and Peter Redgrove

'An important, brave and exciting exploration into territory that belongs to all of us, and nobody could read it without a sense of discovery.' – Margaret Drabble in the *Listener*

THE AMBIVALENCE OF ABORTION
Linda Bird Francke

In interviews with men and women of all ages and social groups, Linda Bird Francke describes the human experience of abortion, and in doing so casts new light on one of the most controversial and complicated issues of our time.

THE CAPTIVE WIFE
Hannah Gavron

'A perceptive and telling account of the lives and difficulties of some young mothers' – *The Times Literary Supplement*

'This momentous book will rank as the contemporary successor to the classic works of Booth and Rowntree; its case histories alone should put paid to those who still assert that there is no longer poverty in Britain' – *Barbara Wooton*

POVERTY IN THE UNITED KINGDOM
A SURVEY OF HOUSEHOLD RESOURCES AND STANDARDS OF LIVING

Peter Townsend

'The chief conclusion of this report is that poverty is more extensive than is generally or officially believed, and has to be understood not only as an inevitable feature of severe social inequality but also as a particular consequence of actions by the rich to preserve and enhance their wealth and so deny it to others ... The extremely unequal distribution of wealth is perhaps the single most notable feature of social conditions in the United Kingdom.'

Professor Townsend's massive and controversial survey is the most comprehensive investigation into poverty and wealth in Britain ever undertaken. It has virtually the scope and prestige of a Royal Commission, and will stand as the seminal work on the subject for years to come.

'Not only presents the results of the most extensive survey of poverty carried out in Britain, but also brings together Townsend's thinking over the last 25 years on the subject of poverty, the position of social minorities, and the role of social institutions. It is a veritable tour de force' – *Guardian*

'The contribution to knowledge and understanding is great indeed, and covers so many topics and correlations that it will provide material for discussion for years to come' – *New Society*